Hooking the Reader is ...
In a word --- intensive
In a library --- invaluable
In a classroom --- informative

Stephen P. Byers
Storyteller / Author / Writing Instructor

This wonderful book does something for me that I've been trying (less completely and systematically) to do for myself. If you are a writer, you need it. If you would like to be a writer, you've got to have it. If you simply like to read, it will leave you dizzy and delighted.

Gene Wolfe
best-selling, award-winning science fiction author

This book of shocking quotes and generous commentary will teach writers to become much better hookers.

Priscilla Cogan
Author of *Winona's Web, Compass of the Heart, Crack at Dusk: Crook of Dawn*

Having problems getting started on that novel? In a new book edited by Sharon Rendell-Smock titled 'HOOKING THE READER; OPENING LINES THAT SELL,' over 100 published authors (including the author of this review) share their secrets for beginning their novel, as well as offering other helpful tips and advice to the aspiring writer. This is a book not only for writers, but for anyone who cares about books and writing. Skillfully laid out for ease of reading, it's both entertaining and informative. Certainly a worthy addition to any writer's bookshelf.

Joan Hall Hovey
Author of *Nowhere to Hide*

Ms. Rendell-Smock has compiled a treasure trove of idea starters for the novice and insights into the process for anyone with an interest in the art and craft of writing. For more seasoned authors, the book provides affirmation that they are not alone in their creative ruminations about the genesis of stories or the labor of putting first words on paper. It was a real pleasure to see the first lines of so many authors in one place for comparison. I was hooked!

Jennifer Blake
Romance Author

HOOKING
THE
READER

Sharon Rendell-Smock

Hooking the Reader: Opening Lines that Sell

First published in 2001

10 9 8 7 6 5 4 3 2 1

PUBLISHER'S NOTE

Individual authors hold copyright to their material.

ISBN 0-9654981-2-3

Author's photograph by Crouch Photography

Book cover by Ruth Frank
http://www.artbyruth.net

Printed in the United States by:
Morris Publishing
3212 East Highway 30
Kearney, NE 68847
1-800-650-7888

Other books by Sharon Rendell-Smock

Living with Big Cats: The Story of Jungle Larry, Safari Jane, and David Tetzlaff

Getting Hooked: Fiction's Opening Sentences 1950s-1990s

Table of Contents

Preface   xv

1 -- Best Sellers: Built One Line at a Time   1

Earl Emerson   2
Peter Lance   3
Priscilla Cogan   5
Dana Stabenow   5
Jean Hager   5
Mark Sumner   6
Off the Shelf   7
Gene Wolfe   9
Scott Mackay   9
Voyle A. Glover   11
L. Sprague de Camp   12
Peter Robinson   13
Janice Steinberg   15
Off the Shelf   16
Les Standiford   18
Edo van Belkom   19
Ralph A. Sperry   19
Jack Williamson   20
Off the Shelf   21

2 -- Grab the Reader in the First Chapter   23

James W. Hall   23
Stuart Woods   24
Mary Balogh   24

Off the Shelf   25

Henry G. Stratmann, M.D.   27

Carol Dennis   28

Martha Bayless   30

Off the Shelf   31

Jane Yolen   33

Justin Leiber   33

Shirley Rousseau Murphy   35

Off the Shelf   37

3 – Techniques to Hook the Reader   41

Laurence Shames   41

Joanne Pence   42

Sasha Miller   43

Russell James   44

John Legg   45

Paul Levinson   46

Off the Shelf   47

Anne McCaffrey   49

Nancy Kress   49

Off the Shelf   50

Courtni Wright   52

Nina Gettler w/a Nina Beaumont   53

John Paxton Sheriff   53

Sara Hoskinson Frommer   54

Terry Brooks   55

Off the Shelf   55

4 -- Do Hooks Matter?   59

Michael Connelly   59
Loren D. Estleman   60
Joan Van Nuys   60
Sir Arthur C. Clarke   61
Margaret (Meg) Chittenden   62
Walter Satterthwait   63
Jonnie Jacobs   64
E. C. Ayres   65
Off the Shelf   66
Marilyn Meredith   68
C. J. Cherryh   69
Michael H. Payne   69
Off the Shelf   70
Ron Goulart   71
Dennis L. McKiernan   73
Denise Turney   75
Frederik Pohl   76
Off the Shelf   77

5 -- Set the Mood   81

Harlen Campbell   81
K.D. Wentworth   82
William Sanders   83
Robert Weinberg   83
Larry Niven   84
Jaclyn Reding   87
Robert J. Sawyer   88
Off the Shelf   89

Edward D. Hoch   91

Greg Bear   91

Barbara Paul   92

William C. Dietz   93

Off the Shelf   93

John Moore   96

Deborah Morgan   96

Carla Peltonen   97

Patricia Eakins   98

Off the Shelf   98

6 -- Writer and Reader Interactions   101

Joe Haldeman   102

Carolyn Wheat   103

Valerie J. Freireich   104

Poul Anderson   105

Charles L. Fontenay   105

Lawrence Watt-Evans   107

Off the Shelf   108

Eileen Kernaghan   110

Mary Rosenblum   111

Martha C. Lawrence   113

David Brin   114

G. David Nordley   115

Off the Shelf   117

Janet Jeppson Asimov   118

M. K. Wren /Martha Kay Renfroe   119

Off the Shelf   121

7 – What about Action?   **123**

    Sarah Smith   **124**

    Claire Delacroix   **125**

    Valerie Wolzien   **127**

    Robert Chase   **127**

    Off the Shelf   **128**

    Steven Womack   **130**

    Joan Hall Hovey   **131**

    Alan Dean Foster   **132**

    Off the Shelf   **132**

    Brian Herbert   **133**

    B. A. Chepaitis   **136**

    Mark L. Van Name   **136**

    Off the Shelf   **137**

8 -- Interest Yourself and Your Reader   **139**

    Jennifer Blake   **139**

    Phyllis Ann Karr   **141**

    Sheila Finch   **143**

    Off the Shelf   **144**

    Lora Roberts   **146**

    Joe R. Lansdale   **148**

    Off the Shelf   **151**

    Frank Thompson   **152**

    Off the Shelf   **154**

9 -- Prologues and Epilogues   **157**

     Fern Michaels   **158**

     Jane Toombs   **159**

     Kate Freiman   **160**

     Off the Shelf   **161**

     Aileen Schumacher   **163**

     Mary Jo Putney   **165**

     Off the Shelf   **166**

     Eileen Putman   **168**

     Charles Wilson   **169**

10 -- Full Circle   **173**

     Lee Harris   **173**

     Laura Lynn Leffers   **174**

     Dean Ing   **176**

     Off the Shelf   **177**

     Tara K. Harper   **180**

     Yvonne Navarro   **182**

     Off the Shelf   **184**

     Ellen Kushner   **187**

     J. A. Lawrence   **188**

     Off the Shelf   **190**

     "The End" -- Promise Fulfilled   **193**

Appendix A – Off the Classic Shelf   **195**

Appendix B – Authors' Awards   **209**

Index   **213**

Preface

The Stars of this Book

For the first time, over one hundred well-known authors give their thoughts on opening sentences. *Hooking the Reader: Opening Lines That Sell* is the first book to bring together thoughts of hundreds of best-selling authors talking about their opening hooks--the many styles of hooks, their construction, humor, dialogue, disparate elements, and their relationship to the story's ending.

These writers generously gave their time and original material to **Hooking the Reader: Opening Lines that Sell**. These authors, known worldwide, collectively have earned every literary award imaginable. Too many to name here, a list of the awards appears in Appendix B.

The authors collectively have written 1,648 individual book titles, selling scores of millions of copies. Aside from this, these people have racked up additional thousands of published short stories, novellas, and co-authored stories.

If publication is not accolade enough, another moment an author treasures is that when his work is translated into a foreign language. Collectively, the titles written by these authors have been translated from English into 42 languages: Afrikaans, Arabic, Bulgarian, Cantonese, Czech, Danish, Dutch, Finnish, Flemish, French, German, Greek, Hawaiian, Hebrew, Hindi, Hungarian, Icelandic, Indonesian, Inuit, Italian, Japanese, Korean, Latvian, Lithuanian, Mandarin, Malay, Norwegian, Pharsee, Polish, Portuguese, Romanian, Russian, Serbo-Croat, Spanish, Slovak, Swedish, Tamil, Togalog, Turkish, Ukrainian, Urdu, and Xhosa!

Both authors and readers are thrilled when a book becomes a movie. The motion picture industry is wholly dependent on books. The warmest and perhaps most profitable award is when one's book becomes a movie (providing the filmmaker can see things the way the author does). A number of the works discussed in this book were scripted for movies, which went on to win movie awards. I won't attempt to name all of those!

Authors have a freedom that many of us seek in choosing where they reside—nationally and internationally—be it from the Texas or Tuscaloosa, sunny Florida, romantic Sri Lanka, Manhattan, Malibu, Madagascar, London, Rome or Costa Rica. The world is theirs.

The Story Behind the Book

Fiction's first sentences always intrigued me. For years when I found an interesting one, I jotted it down. I began to wonder whether other readers would be interested in **what grabs the reader**. Thus, I wrote the first version of this book (*Getting Hooked: Fiction's Opening Sentences 1950s-1990s*), which contains opening sentences, sidebars, and, divided by topic and decade, some history of what was going on in the world during the time the works were created. It demonstrated similarities and differences between the times. Uncanny as it is, many of the sentences written in the 1950s are true today, a prime example being:

> **Most people won't even open the door when someone rings their bell.**
> Harold Q. Masur, *So Rich, So Lovely and So Dead*, 1952

After *Getting Hooked* was published, it was obvious that a much richer arena had opened up. I asked authors what they thought of some of their first sentences; to provide some of their own favorites and how they came up with them; and in general, their thought processes when creating those sentences. Many volunteered a paragraph; others contributed a page or more, taking whatever path they wished. Their generosity and willing responses proved the axiom that writers are warm and eager to help each other.

Even though a very few authors had to have their copyrights listed specifically, I want to make it clear that each author, contributing to this book, holds his or her own copyright of the material.

After receiving much of the original material on openers, I looked for patterns. What fit together? By using that approach I determined the chapter titles and drew each chapter into a whole, developing detailed introductions.

This book is intended as a source of both amusement and serious contemplation--for readers, fans, and writers.

Format

Insights Each of the book's ten chapters has the following components:

- **Introduction** – I introduce each chapter.
  In these sections, the authors divulge their thoughts about Opening sentences and give examples of their favorites. Authors' Internet web sites, whenever available, are listed with the author's name.

- **Off the Shelf** – For these sections, I present arresting opening lines by successful fiction writers–hundreds of examples from mystery, science fiction, romance, western, and mainstream. (Obviously, the opening lines in this book cannot be comprehensive.)

- **Sidebars** – I mix light-hearted tidbits and serious facts throughout the book.

Fiction (fik shen) n. The class of literature comprising works of imaginative narration, especially in prose form (*Webster's Encyclopedic Unabridged Dictionary of the English Language*)

All fiction basically follows one blueprint: setting, plot and usually a subplot, tension between characters, and resolution.

Details of place and time period must be true to life. A passage referring to legalized gambling in Washington, D.C., unless set in the timeframe of the future, would destroy an author's credibility.

Beyond fiction's shared aspects, mystery, science fiction, western, and romance all have their own genre-specific story pattern.

Mystery: may take place in any time period and setting. Heroes/heroines hold a variety of occupations, such as investigator, detective, police officer, coroner, psychologist, salvage consultant, retired bookkeeper, attorney, bank officer, and even housewife. The plot may involve staking out, tailing, blackmailing, kidnapping, and murdering by many methods. Realism is crucial to these suspense/thriller tales.

The fictionalized detective of the 40s and 50s got his start in the dime novels and pulp magazines of 1910-1930, such as *Black Mask*, *Dime Detective*, *Clues*, *Bulldog Drummond*, and *Detective Story*. The hard-boiled detective's style was fast-talking, fast shooting, cocky.

In just one novel the writer may incorporate story lines that cover the psychological makeup of criminals, corruption, the environment, and pollution. Some use social satire to drive home a point.

Many mystery writers portray their concern about our environment. However, this isn't the only ecology-minded field. Mystery and science fiction share many such themes.

Science fiction: Settings vary from galaxies, parallel universes, robots, and androids, to aliens and other weird creatures. Themes often involve utopia, colonization of other worlds, time travel (in the past, present, or near or far future), paranoia, invisibility, evolution, overpopulation, and immortality, which sometimes included cryonic preservation and other mysterious carryings-on.

Science fiction also has its own terminology. However, the stories usually are based on fact, such as the known distances between planets. Credibility is the desired goal.

The Western: Set in the Old West, and occasionally Africa, Latin America, Australia, or other frontiers, characters include trappers, white hunters, cowboys, mountaineers, Royal Canadian Mounties, and Indians. Westerns thrive on conflicts between men, rugged individuals of all descriptions, and between man and nature. Again, timeframe must be accurate: aficionados will know when a Winchester 98-lever action or a Buntline Special was invented.

Romance: The realistic historical time period is often contemporary or Gothic. Common settings are war, Medieval times, plantations, and the south. Characters run the gamut from pirates and their loose women, to knights in shining armor and their heroic ladies, Victorian rakes and cads, and the beauties finding fulfillment in the arms of handsome, wealthy lovers. The plot can portray the heroine married to a man with a secret, or an orphan maiden involved with the man of the house. Plots often involve graphic action, violence, passion, and fainting.

****

Most authors agree that the first sentence is the hardest. Often they are the last words they write.

Sharon Rendell-Smock
Space Coast, FL
http://www.rendell-smock.com

Acknowledgments

My heartfelt thanks to my friend Gene Wolfe, an inspiring man. He was the first author I told about my idea for this book. Not only was he excited about the topic; he was the first one to contribute his time to put on paper his thoughts about opening sentences.

I am thankful to every author in this book. These authors' kindness and generosity in creating original material at my request can't be surpassed: Poul Anderson, Janet Jeppson Asimov, E.C. Ayres, Mary Balough, Martha Bayless, Greg Bear, Nina Beaumont, Jennifer Blake, David Brin, Terry Brooks, Harlen Campbell, Robert Chase, B. A. Chepaitis, C. J. Cherryh, Margaret Chittenden, Sir Arthur C. Clarke, Priscilla Cogan, Michael Connelly, L. Sprague deCamp, Claire Delacroix, Carol Dennis, William C. Dietz, Patricia Eakins, Earl Emerson, Loren D. Estleman, Sheila Finch, Charles L. Fontenay, Alan Dean Foster, Kate Freiman, Valerie J. Freireich, Sara Hoskinson Frommer, Voyle A. Glover, Ron Goulart, Jean Hager, Joe Haldeman, James W. Hall, Tara K. Harper, Lee Harris, Brian Herbert, Edward D. Hoch, Joan Hall Hovey, Dean Ing, Jonnie Jacobs, Russell James, Phyllis Ann Karr, Eileen Kernaghan, Nancy Kress, Ellen Kushner, Joe R. Lansdale, Peter Lance, J. A. Lawrence, Martha C. Lawrence, Laura Lynn Leffers, John Legg, Justin Leiber, Paul Levinson, Scott Mackay, Anne McCaffrey, Dennis L. McKiernan, Marilyn Meredith, Fern Michaels, Sasha Miller, John Moore, Deborah Morgan, Shirley Rousseau Murphy, Yvonne Navarro, Larry Niven, G. David Nordley, Barbara Paul, Michael H. Payne, Carla Peltonen and Molly Swanton (the writing team Lynn Erickson), Joanne Pence, Frederik Pohl, Eileen Putman, Mary Jo Putney, Jaclyn Reding, M.K. Wren /Martha Kay Renfroe, Lora Roberts, Peter Robinson, Mary Rosenblum, William Sanders, Walter Satterthwait, Robert J. Sawyer, Aileen Schumacher, Laurence Shames, John Paxton Sheriff, Sarah Smith, Ralph A. Sperry, Dana Stabenow, Les Standiford, Janice Steinberg, H. G. Stratmann, Mark Sumner, Frank Thompson, Jane Toombs, Denise Turney, Edo van Belkom, Mark L. Van Name, Joan Van Nuys, Lawrence Watt-Evans, Robert Weinberg, K. D. Wentworth, Carolyn Wheat, Jack Williamson, Charles Wilson, Gene Wolfe, Valerie Wolzien, Steven Womack, Stuart Woods, Courtni Wright, and Jane Yolen.

My research for outstanding opening lines began at my bookcases. I supplemented the research at several libraries. A special thanks goes to the helpful staff of these Florida libraries: From the Sarasota County Libraries: Selby Public Library, North Port Public Library, and the Elsie Quirk Public Library; and From the Brevard Library System, the Melbourne Public Library, and the Eau Gallie Library.

A very special thanks to my son, Paul, a wonderful researcher and the best son ever.

1 -- Best Sellers: Built One Line at a Time

Books can start with a bang or a whimper, jarring drama, disruptions, rhythm, contradictions, the unexpected, suspension of disbelief. Authors agree, as in life, first impressions are crucial.

An author's first sentence begins a relationship between the reader and author that lasts in the voyage to reach mutual satisfaction. By the end of the book, it is *their* book. It all begins with words that convince both of them that the time with the book is well spent.

A hook thrown in for effect, having nothing to do with the subsequent story will not do justice to the reader. The opening must lay the groundwork in the perfect way to entice the reader to continue with that book. The opening chapter should hint at the conflict and theme to come.

An authors' roundtable discussion would bring a consensus that the first words are the most important ones you can write. Many authors agree that the first sentence is the hardest, and often the last words they write. In fact, they swear that their characters frequently take over telling the tale.

A story is a living thing. When the characters take over the book, they smooth the story's telling, easing the author's task. At other times, it results in delightful fun or near paranoia, when the cast interferes and takes over the story—conceivably through deliberately twisting the writer's thoughts.

Insights

Earl Emerson

Whether as a reader or an author, it has always been my belief that the first few lines of a book are the most important. I was challenged on this point once by another writer who said, "Why worry so much over the beginning? It takes people hours to read a book. By the time they get to the end, they'll barely remember the opening." Maybe so, but in a world where people have less and less time for leisure reading, if you don't set the hook in the first few sentences, your book might not be read.

There are two ways to set the hook. One is by coming up with an improbable or intriguing story gambit. The second is to open with a rather tame scene but describe it in an unexpected or humorous manner. I've done both. Sometimes well. Sometimes not quite as well.

When I was half finished with the first draft of *Fat Tuesday*, I realized that the first few lines of chapter twelve were snappier than the book's opening. The discovery disturbed me. After days spent tweaking the opening paragraphs I realized I was not going to come up with a better opening. A careful restructuring of the plot turned chapter twelve into chapter one. Here's the opening.

> **I was trapped in a house with a lawyer, a bare-breasted woman and a dead man. The rattlesnake in the paper sack only complicated matters.**

It's what I call a loud beginning. It draws attention to itself. These days I tend to prefer a quieter opening. Here is the opening to *Going Crazy in Public*:

> **Fontana was standing on the roof of the elementary school with his hands in his pockets, thinking that when it came to mouth-to-mouth resuscitation on dogs you could just count him out.**

Quiet or noisy, whether reading or writing, the beginning is my favorite part.

Peter Lance
http://www.firstdegreeburn.com

I cut my teeth in the news business where the five-point lead was God. If you didn't get them into the story in the first graph, they were gone. So when I set out to write my first novel, a film-noir mystery called *First Degree Burn*, I went to Barnes & Noble and read the opening lines from two dozen authors.

I was struck by the fact that a lot of the top-shelf people like Grisham and Cornwell didn't seem to care so much about how they opened. Maybe by the time I found them they didn't have to. But I was mindful of something one of my old bosses at ABC News used to say: "You've got to get them into the tent before you preach to them." So I spent a lot of time on my opening line.

Ironically, the one that was in the manuscript that sold, was not the opening line in the published novel. When the ink was still wet from the printer on my first pass, the open to the book went like this:

> **It was hard enough for Alex to squeeze into the leather bustier, but the four-inch heels were murder. Carlos had been buying her leather and silk outfits for weeks now; form-fitting, cinched at the waist, with ties up the back. Whore clothes. Mostly black, with garters, tiny satin G-strings, and platform spikes. Clothes that pushed her breasts out and her ass up and made her walk in tiny baby steps to the bed.**

That's the way it started at first. Then the book sold. It's a thriller and the hero is a Fire Marshal for the FDNY in New York. I had made up most of the fire stuff when I wrote it on spec. But when it sold, I figured I'd better get to The City and hook up with the real guys. Do some research before I embarrassed myself.

I lucked out by meeting the man who is now New York City's Chief Fire Marshal. Over many beers he took a liking to me and I spent weeks walking in and out of fire scenes with him. He taught me everything. After the book got published, veteran firefighters would come up to me at signings and ask "how long have you been on the job?"

Anyway, in the course of my Jedi training my Master told me a story about a legendary torch in New York they called Superman. He got the name after my guy tried to arrest him on the sixth floor of a building and he jumped out the window. The arsonist fell six stories to the alley below but walked away with a fractured ankle. After that, he got cocky and started calling himself after the Man of Steel.

So, when I got back and decided to rewrite the book, I changed the open... moved Alex and her spikes down a few chapters and started like this...

> **Superman pulled up to the decrepit rowhouse in a black '78 Econoline van. The needles crunched on the sidewalk along Avenue C when he got out. It was a piss-numbing sub-zero night down in Alphabet City, and at half past two in the morning, the streets were dead. Superman looked around before he slid the van door open. There was enough gasoline inside to take down a city block.**

That's how the book appeared on the shelves.

Something must have clicked, because it sold out of its first 55,000 print run and hit the Ingram A-List: The Top 50 Titles In Mystery/Detective Fiction. Ten weeks after publication, my little paperback original was No. 35, right behind the trade edition of L.A. Confidential the week the movie opened. Some of the success came from firefighter word of mouth... some from the starred review in Publisher's Weekly.

But I'll bet a lot of it came from the browsers who picked up the book on the shelves, read the open and decided to "get burned."

Priscilla Cogan
http://www.twocanoespress.com

My first novel, *Winona's Web* (1997) began with these sentences:

When and where the heart can celebrate each awakening day--that becomes home. When and where the spirit can mine for nourishment in the little moments--that becomes home. When and where the mind can distill meaning from the shadows as well as the light--that also becomes home.

It's a lyrical opening that sets readers' expectations that the book is going to focus on joy, spiritual matters, and the derivation of life's purposes. It is also a jarring, ungrammatical beginning - setting up when and where, time and space, process and context as the subjects that will lead us home. And, deep down in all of us, there is a tremendous drive to find our way home--wherever and whenever that may be. The lines seduce the ear but jar the eye-- and that makes for the delicious conflict that is at the center of all good drama.

Dana Stabenow
http://www.stabenow.com

Mickey Spillane said "The first line sells the rest of the book," and he's right, even if I don't always follow his dictum. One of my favorite first lines is from *Blood Will Tell*, the sixth Kate Shugak novel.

The bad news was the blood in her hair.

I was hoping the reader would think, "So, what's the good news?"

Jean Hager

"Start on the day that is different." It's an old saw, but still good advice. In fact, starting the very moment when things change, when the status quo is interrupted, is even better. I've used several types of openings for my mysteries, but the best ones start with a character confronted by a problem that must be dealt with now. *Blooming Murder*, the first book in my Iris House Bed and Breakfast mystery series published by Avon Books, starts this way:

> **A click as soft as a whisper broke the silence of the April night. Tess Darcy awoke abruptly, aware that a sound had roused her from the deep sleep of exhaustion.**

And *Sew Deadly*, another book in the Iris House series starts like this:

> **"I'm going to kill her!" Ross Dellin shouted as he barreled into the room.**

Mark Sumner
www.inlink.com/~range

I **love** a good first line. Here are a few of the things I've used to crank up a fantasy, science fiction or a novel:

Devil's Tower:

> **The shaman came to town near sunset, riding a dead horse.**

From SF/Mystery novel *Insanity, Illinois*:

> **The iguana wore glitter.**

See No Weevil, written under the pen name "Kenyon Morr:"

> **Rosella sneezed. Not a small, dainty sneeze as was proper for a princess, but a great snot-slinging nose honker.**

The Monster of Minnesota:

> **"Yeah, so what happened after Elvis shot the dinosaur?"**

Devil's Engine:

> **The storm rolled in from the west and the wagon ran before it.**

From the short story "Leather Doll:"

> **Lisle was a Hereford, born for meat and leather.**

From the novel *Vampires of Vermont*:

> **"Count Dracula's on line two and he's pissed."**

Obviously, a good first line must be "hooky" -- it has to give the reader a reason to get to line two -- but a good first line also sets tone, establishes place, even defines an arc that it takes the next twenty thousand lines to complete. A first line is a promise between an author and a reader. "This is my offer to you. This is a slice of my world and a taste of how I will deliver it to you. Interested in another bite?" An ideal first line is not just clever; it's also a -good line- in the sense of being a seamless part of the rest of the work.

Off the Shelf

Some of the winning lines, then back to what the experts say.

We were about to give up and call it a night when somebody dropped the girl off the bridge.
John D. MacDonald, *Darker Than Amber*, 1966

I know an old couple who live near Hell.
Gene Wolfe, *Bed and Breakfast*, 1995

The Latin term *pro bono*, as most attorneys will attest, roughly translated means *for boneheads* and applies to work done without charge. Not that I practice law, but I am usually smart enough to avoid having to donate my services. In this case, my client was in a coma, which made billing a trick.
Sue Grafton, *"O" is for Outlaw*, 1999

Sudden death saved his life.
Edna Buchanan, *Pulse*, 1998

"Reservation?" said Sam Katz. "Whaddya mean, you have a reservation? This is my house."
Laurence Shames, *Mangrove Squeeze*, 1998

In 1982, when she was seventy-two years old, Lily Roberts Maynard published her first book.
Sue Miller, *The Distinguished Guest*, 1995

The most appalling feature of the morning after I nearly committed adultery was my lack of surprise.
Susan Howatch, *Ultimate Prizes*, 1989

There was no getting around it. Edna Ellett had picked an impossible week to die.
Sara Hoskinson Frommer, *Buried in Quilts*, 1994

It would be easy to say we resented Earl Dietrich because he was rich.
James Lee Burke, *Heartwood*, 1999

Millions upon millions of years ago, when the continents were already formed and the principal features of the earth had been decided, there existed, then as now, one aspect of the world that dwarfed all others.
James A. Michener, *Hawaii*, 1959

The greatest part of a writer's time is spent in reading, in order to write; a man will turn over half a library to make one book.

Samuel Johnson, in Boswell's *Life*, 1775

Insights

Gene Wolfe

From one of my favorites, *A Criminal Proceeding* ©:

Two days before Easter Sunday, at eleven forty-three p.m., Stephen Brodie's apartment door was broken down by a mixed force comprised of elements from the New York and Philadelphia police departments, the Secret Service, the Federal Bureau of Investigation, the Bureau of Narcotics, CBS, ABC, and the *Washington Post*.

I think it was Jack Woodford who said that the way to begin a Western novel was to shoot the sheriff on page 1. You can begin a book effectively without shooting the sheriff, of course. It's harder, but it can be done. That is good advice for anyone smart enough to realize that "shoot" and "sheriff" are metaphors. What Jack Woodford (a pseudonym) was saying was that people are interested in disruptions of the normal order—something violently, or subtly, or oddly amiss. I have been reading Tony Hillerman's *Skinwalkers*, and it begins with the strange behavior of a cat. The idea is the same; in my story, Brodie is not simply arrested, his arrest is a media event, like the storming of the Branch Davidian Compound by BATF.

But the thing that sets this opening apart is the date; many readers have been sharp enough to catch it and say oh-ho!"

Scott Mackay

I begin with an opener of my own, from my science fiction novel, *Outpost*:

Seventeen years old, and she couldn't remember murdering anyone, couldn't remember a trial or sentencing, or who, exactly, she had murdered.

I think openers have to do more than just hook the reader. They must convince the reader that the writer can write, that he's a credible narrative guide, and that he's going to offer the reader something different. Anybody can shoot the sheriff in the first sentence, but I believe an opener has to go further. An opener has to be crafted, not dashed off. Every single word has to be looked at carefully. The openers I like best are ones where disparate and unexpected elements are juxtaposed one against the other.

In my own opener above, the disparate elements play off each other to create interest. Seventeen year old girls usually don't murder, and if they do, they more than likely remember who they kill. The unusual and unexpected, I think, is a cornerstone of the great opener. Take the opening sentence from Larry McMurtry's *Lonesome Dove*:

> **When Augustus came out on the porch, the blue pigs were eating a rattlesnake—not a very big one.**

Blue pigs eating a rattlesnake. Unusual, and in this case, striking. No questions raised, no sheriffs shot, no mysteries to solve, but who cares when you have blue pigs eating rattlesnakes? You want to read on.

From Anthony Burgess' *Earthly Powers*:

> **It was the afternoon of my eighty-first birthday, and I was in bed with my catamite when Ali announced that the archbishop had come to see me.**

Man in bed with boy prostitute when Moslem servant announces a Catholic official at the door. The disparate elements immediately draw you in, to say nothing of the situation.

Finally, this age-old standby, by anonymous:

> **"Take your hand off my knee," said the Queen to the plumber.**

Same thing. The disparate elements draw you in. If a writer does something unusual with his first sentence, something I've never seen before, combining elements that take me by surprise, be it blue pigs and rattlesnakes, or Queens and plumbers, he'll have my reading dollar, no questions asked—and no sheriffs shot for that matter either.

Voyle A. Glover
http://brevia.com/Main/stories.htm

Opening from my short story entitled "Goin' to Texas":

I cut him wide and deep and it hurt him bad, I know, because I could see the pain on his face. There was surprise there, too, probably on account of me being just a kid to him, a growed man, tall as tree to me. But I grew up fast in the hills of Tennessee and there's some folk there who'd cut you quicker'n a wolf can swallow raw meat. I ain't braggin', but I got to be known there as someone not to trouble. This man thought he could kick me like I was a saloon dog in his way. He'd live, but he'd hurt a long time, unless he figured to use that Navy Colt .36 on his leg.

Openings in a story are everything. It is usually there where you'll either hook the reader or lose them. If you begin your story by boring your reader, he or she is likely to assume (perhaps incorrectly) that the rest of the read is going to be as slow and dull as the beginning. So it is imperative for the author to grasp the mind of the reader and compel the reader to turn the page.

Louis L'Amour, the Dean of Western Fiction, felt that the art of writing good western fiction was "telling a good yarn," and he was excellent at story-telling. "I strive to tell a good story, right from the get-go. If I don't open with action, I usually will open with an individual who is bound to whet the appetite of the reader to learn more of this person. It also has to be an opening scene that is pregnant with possibilities, usually, in a western, a confrontation of some sort, an opportunity to define the hero as 'one tough hombre.' Western readers love their heroes to be just that: heroes."

L. Sprague de Camp

www.lspraguedecamp.com

Editor's note: Sprague was greatly bereaved when his beloved wife of sixty years, Catherine, passed away April 9, 2000. Sprague followed her, passing on November 6, 2000. I appreciate that he shared some of his last words on writing.

The Reluctant King published by Baen in October 1996. *The Reluctant King* is the complete trilogy of previously published volumes: *The Goblin Tower*, c 1968, *The Clocks of Iraz*, c 1971 and *The Unbeheaded King*, c 1983

The opening lines from: The Reluctant King The Goblin Tower:

> **"A curious custom," said the barbarian, "to cut off your king's head every five years. I wonder your throne finds any takers!"**
>
> **On the scaffold, the headsman brushed a whetstone along the gleaming edge of his ax, dropped the stone into his pouch, squinted along the blade, and touched it here and there with his thumb. Those in the crowd below could not see his satisfied smile because of the black hood, which - save for the eyeholes - covered his head. The ax was neither a woodcutter's tool nor a warrior's weapon. Whereas its helve, carven of good brown oak, was that of a normal ax, its blue steelhead was unwontedly broad, like a butcher's cleaver.**

These opening lines seemed like a good way to start, with a contradiction. How could a king govern without a head? It would make him permanently incapable of performing the duties of a king.

In 1950-51, I wrote *The Tritonian Ring* in my first flush of enthusiasm for Robert Howard's sword-and-sorcery fiction. Like Howard and Tolkien, I had laid my scene in our world in prehistoric times. The book has been through several editions.

In 1966 I came back to heroic fantasy, starting *The Goblin Tower*. Pyramid Books brought out the novel in 1968. The title comes from a ruined castle Catherine and I saw in the U.K. in 1963, of which the guidebook identified one feature as "The Goblin Tower," without explanation of this curious name. I made it a castle built of real goblins, turned into stones.

The opening sequence, where King Jorian is about to have his head cut off and thrown up for grabs, is based upon Frazer's *Golden Bough*. Frazer tells of a kingdom in Malabar, India, where the ruler (actually the Prime Minister) is periodically beheaded, and his successor was he who caught the head.

Peter Robinson
http://www.interlog.com/~peterob/home.html

The rhythm of the first sentence interests me, perhaps because I have a background in poetry and I find that rhythm has resonance. I have always been proud of the opening sentence of my first book, *Gallows View*-not so much because it's an interesting image, but because it's iambic hexameter! Of course, if the rhythm is used to express an interesting image, so much the better.

The woman stepped into a circle of light and began to undress.

I like contrasts, echoes, and images that rub against one another, or jar together. The opening sentence of my forthcoming Inspector Banks book, *In a Dry Season*, reads:

It was the Summer of Love and I had just buried my husband when I first went back to visit the reservoir that had flooded my childhood village.

A bit long, perhaps, but it packs a lot in. It indicates the different time frames the novel will deal with, hints at mystery and contrasts "Summer of Love" with "buried my husband." It also indicates in its rhythm the elegiac tone that infuses much of the novel.

On the whole, though, I am probably far more interested in the opening paragraph or scene , in setting a mood, than I am in coming up with a surprising or shocking opening sentence. Often my books open with the scene of the crime, and it's quite a challenge to come up with interesting variations on this old chestnut. The same contrasts and echoes can be developed in a scene, however, as I tried to do in the opening scene of *Innocent Graves*, where a minister's wife wanders drunk in a graveyard and finds the body of a young girl beside a statue of an angel.

Literary echoes can also work on occasion. If you don't get them, it doesn't matter, but if you do, they can add an extra dimension to your reading pleasure. Also in *Innocent Graves*, I deliberately echoed Dickens's opening to *Bleak House* because you can hardly begin a book set in the fog without doing that!

> **The night it all began, a thick fog rolled down the dale and enfolded the town of Eastvale in its shroud.**

Again, there's a certain eerie rhythm to it, which also sets the mood. And what, I hope the reader wonders, is this mysterious "it" that all began?

Dialogue can be particularly useful for openings, especially if you appear to start in mid conversation so that the readers gets the sense of some mysterious exchange already having gone on. I used this in the Banks short story "Summer Rain," where Detective Constable Susan Gay asks, **"And exactly how many times have you died, Mr. Singer?"**

Short stories are both a challenge and a liberation. Openings that perhaps wouldn't work so well in a Banks novel can work there. Sometimes it's fun to do something different in a short story, such as go for a comic effect. Again, this can often be achieved by yoking together incongruous images, such as this one from "Some Land in Florida":

> **The morning they found Santa Claus floating face down in the pool, I had a hangover of gargantuan proportions.**

This was a story that actually came from the odd experience of sitting in the Florida sunshine close to Christmas and listening to a man in a Santa suit lead the elderly condo residents in "White

Christmas" and "Rudolf the Red-Nosed Reindeer" by the swimming pool. He was playing an electric piano, which in the story, needless to say, ends up along with him in the pool--still plugged in!

Janice Steinberg
www.janicesteinberg.com

The opening of a book is so crucial that I teach a workshop devoted to the subject. I call it "Killer Hooks." In the workshop, I cover the major types of hooks used in mystery fiction: action or a compelling situation, a character who's unusual and/or in trouble, and powerful descriptive language. I share some of my favorite openings, like Minette Walters' hideously brilliant character sketch in *The Sculptress* and James Lee Burke's exquisite descriptive prose. In both of these cases, the authors combine the more literary hooks with a dramatic situation; for instance, Burke juxtaposes a sky "the color of torn plums" and a jarring, not at all lyrical setting-Angola penitentiary.

About half of the workshop focuses on the students' work. I invite them to read the first pages of stories they're writing. One page only! Because if they haven't hooked the reader by the end of the first page, they've lost their chance. I've noticed a common problem in openings by student writers. They know they have two important tasks at the start of a story: to introduce the protagonist and get the action going. Many students start out by describing their protagonist, getting into that detailed (but not all that gripping) back story they spent hours developing about the protagonist's childhood, family, favorite color, and so on. But they haven't provided any compelling situation to make the reader care what happens to this person!

I struggled with a problem like this in the opening of *Death in a City of Mystics*. In my first draft, a character was standing on a hill, overlooking an ancient cemetery. The sun was setting. There was a lovely, lyrical atmosphere. The bad news: the character was completely passive.

Here's the version I eventually submitted to my publisher:

The snakes! Didn't anybody warn them about the snakes?

Standing at the edge of the Old City, the American woman called to the three young tourists walking-bare-legged, shod only in sandals-in the ancient cemetery below her.

"Hey!" She waved at them. "Hey!"

One of the three, a girl, glanced up. She looked scarcely older than the woman's teenage granddaughter.

"Snakes! There are snakes!" the woman yelled in English and then Hebrew, jabbing her finger toward the ground.

The focus is on the imminent threat. But by showing the character in action, I managed to let the reader know a great deal about her: That she's the kind of person who gets involved; she sees someone in danger and immediately responds. That she's old enough to have a teenage granddaughter. I also told the reader that this is taking place in an exotic locale. After I had dealt with the danger, then I allowed myself to bring in the more lyrical, descriptive writing from my first draft.

Off the Shelf

Like everybody else, he wanted a handout.
Bruno Fischer, *Run for Your Life*, 1953

Marrakech is just what the guidebooks say it is.
Len Deighton, *Horse Under Water*, 1963

One thing I've learned is that strange things do happen.
Alice Hoffman, *Local Girls*, 1999

At approximately ten-forty-five, Della Street nervously began looking at her wrist watch.
Erle Stanley Gardner, *The Case of the Stepdaughter's Secret*, 1963

Fontana liked to think he wasn't a murderer.
Earl W. Emerson, *Black Hearts and Slow Dancing*, 1988

When Menolly, daughter of Yanus Sea Holder, arrived at the Harper Craft Hall, she came in style, aboard a bronze dragon.
Anne McCaffrey, *Dragonsinger*, 1977

They say I'm dead.
Herbert Lieberman, *The Climate of Hell*, 1978

Gynecologists lie.
Gail Parent, *The Best Laid Plans*, 1980

He hurried out of the lighted foyer of the church into the cool night, hoping that the girl with the insolent red mouth had waited for him.
Wade Miller, *Devil May Care*, 1950

He was of medium height, somewhat chubby, and good looking with curly red hair and an innocent gay face, more remarkable for a humorous air about the eyes and large mouth than for any strength of chin or nobility of nose.
Harmon Wouk, *The Caine Mutiny*, 1951

Detective Bert Kling went outside to throw up.
Ed McBain, *Shotgun*, 1969
The first time he saw her, he simply knew.
Lisa Gardner, *The Perfect Husband,* 1998

I'm the vampire Lestat.
Anne Rice, *The Queen of the Damned*, 1988

Hell at its worst couldn't top an Oklahoma summer day.
Giles A. Lutz, *The Great Railroad War*, 1981

An angry deity glowered at Alex.
David Brin, *Earth*, 1990

Have you ever known a famous man before he became famous?
Herman Wouk, *Youngblood Hawke*, 1962

Truman Capote on the editing process:

"I believe more in scissors than I do in the pencil."

Insights

Les Standiford
Info on the Creative Writing Program at FIU is at www.fiu.edu

Yes, opening lines are crucial: Think how many impressions are formed in your mind when a person you've never seen before walks into a room, or responds to you during an introduction. Rightly or wrongly, you know almost immediately whether or not this is someone you want to get to know further, for that is simply human nature. Actors labor endlessly to fashion just the right "entrance" onto stage--and it should be the same way for writers of fiction. That first sentence or two makes the first real impression. The first sentence should make a reader want to come in, the last should make the reader want to come back. In a very real sense, that first sentence should be a microcosm, as nearly as you can make it so, of the whole of the book that follows: its style of course, but also character, place, mood, and subject, insofar as is possible, (and always dependent upon your strategy for the opening.) Here's the opening sentence of the first in the John Deal series (now totaling five volumes): *Done Deal*:

> **Manolo Reyes glanced at his watch, a digital model with Drakkar printed across its face, then looked out the office window, across the deserted service bays of the station. The afternoon thunderheads had passed over, but the sun was dying, sinking into the Everglades a few miles west.**

As Manolo will himself soon sink, poor bastard. And if the reader doesn't know that for certain, there is surely a strong suggestion of what is to come, or so I hope. You see two sentences there, strictly speaking, but I could just as well have put a colon after station. In any case, I hope I've not only suggested something of where this is headed, but also conveyed something of this character's status and his surroundings. And most importantly, I hope I have established the rhythms of the prose, the kind of music, if you will, that I will be playing throughout. Maybe not as pithy as "Call me Ishmael," but I'm still learning.

Edo van Belkom

www.geocities.com/SoHo/Nook/6877/

> **There was nothing wrong with Samuel Goldman's memory.**
> **Not really.** *Baseball Memories*

> **My husband died during childbirth.** *S.P.S.*

The biggest hurdle a writer of speculative fiction faces is suspension of disbelief. In simplest terms, suspension of disbelief means that the reader is willing to believe whatever happens in the story is in fact possible. The first lines from "Baseball Memories" and "S.P.S" both start to work on the reader's suspension of disbelief as soon as they begin the story so that by the time they're asked to believe the part that's truly incredible, they've had plenty of warning that things are different in the universe that the story is taking place in.

Ralph A. Sperry

http://www.alexlit.com

Unless you're attempting something like *Finnegan's Wake*, the hardest part of writing any fiction is the opening sentence because it's the first impression you make on the reader, so, naturally, you want it to be good. And if it's a killer sentence, that's terrific, but something that happens rather infrequently in my experience. Longer stories, and especially novels, tend to be too complex to be captured by a single, trenchant statement. So I usually rely on an opening paragraph, which is the second hardest part of writing.

But one of my good, if not necessarily killer, opening sentences begins the SF story, "History," which deals with a middle-aged archaeologist who falls for someone who turns out to be an alien being:

> **He was unscientifically infatuated with her -- this statuesque, russet-haired, golden-eyed woman who served as on-site liaison for the corporation funding his dig.**

Another comes from my mainstream story, "The Middle Class," which is set in Brazil, and is basically a character study of a woman whose future was ruined by her country's unstable economy:

She had a pretty face made thin by an accumulation of losses.

In both cases, what matters as much as anything is the rhythm of the words, which, I hope, engages the mind, and carries the reader into the story.

As I said, however, opening paragraphs usually work better for me. For example, my SF story, "On Vacation," which uses a form that's sometimes referred to as the "British" short story, because it has both a main plot and a fully developed subplot:

Once upon a time, on a planet far, far away, a young Aten man named Karfas Proklin was employed on the Starship Project. His duties involved the installation of environmental systems. But being handy, he was often asked to work on navigation equipment, too. His friends called him Karfi.

This does begin with a telling allusion, of course, but relies primarily on a brief, descriptive progression that ends abruptly with the simplicity of the final sentence. Rhythm also matters here, but in a more conceptual way. Thus, the effective opening sentence isn't the first, although it sets a tone, but the last, which brings the character quickly into personal focus by introducing his nickname.

Jack Williamson

The opening sentence of my early novel, *The Green Girl*, has sometimes been reprinted as an example (though there are stories that might need a more subtle approach).

At high noon on May 4, 1999, the sun went out.

In a handout for student writers about what should go in the first page of a manuscript, I comment that submissions from unknowns go into a slush pile that is sorted through by a busy editor who may not look beyond the dozen lines of copy on the first page. The challenge to the writer is to get him or her to look at page 2.

A good opening gives the reader a bridge from his own world to the new or different world of the story. A couple more attempts at that. The first line from my first story, "The Metal Man."

> **The metal man stands in a dusty corner of the Tyburn College museum.**

The metal man introduces the world of the story, but small college museums exist in the reader's world.

> **She hit Portales like a falling star.**

The first line from my most recent story, "Miss Million." Portales is the small college town where I live. Miss Million is a time traveler from the far future. "Falling star" seemed a fit symbol for her. She is something out of the unknown. Falling stars are transient; so is she. The tone of the story is light, not melodramatic, though to me the theme is serious.

Off the Shelf

The world had teeth and it could bite you with them anytime it wanted.
Stephen King, *The Girl Who Loved Tom Gordon*, 1999

"If you want to make a good impression on people, my father used to say, be a listener, not a talker."
Stephen Birmingham, *Shades of Fortune*, 1989

Nola lay facedown on her bed, staring at the knife in her hand.
Piers Anthony and Julie Brady, *Dream a Little Dream*, 1999

They said a child had died in the attic.
Anne Rice, *The Vampire Armand*, 1998

All I had to do to earn some dough was kill a guy.
Bruno Fischer, *The Fast Buck*, 1952

"At first, they were saying about him, Oh, my God. It's Hitler all over again!"
William F. Buckley, Jr., *Stained Glass*, 1978

It was the laughter that made her run, more than the dark, more than that gliding shadow.
Whitley Strieber, *Unholy Fire*, 1992

"You said you would never go back," Cressida reminded me.
Anna Gilbert, *A Walk in the Wood*, 1989

There were parts of Kansas City where you could get your head caved in or your ribs parted by a sharp knife in broad daylight.
John Reese, *The Cherokee Diamondback*, 1977

For as long as I could remember, the only person I could share my deepest secrets with was Luke Casteel Jr.
V.C. Andrews, *Gates of Paradise*, 1989

Wade Mattlock lay on the cold ground wishing he had paid closer attention to the old Indian woman's instructions in Kansas.
Johnny Mullins, *Wade's Last Gunfight*, 1987

Burned out at thirty-two, she'd had enough.
Steve Martini, *Critical Mass*, 1998

The joke in the Starfleet is that the only thing that can travel faster than warp 10 is news.
Diane Duane, *Spock's World*, 1988

He had stopped last night in the Gunsight Hills making dry camp because others had reached the water hole before him and he preferred to avoid other travelers.
Louis L'Amour, *Last Stand at Popago Wells*, 1957

When Oliver saw his sister in her bridesmaid's dress he laughed so much he could hardly stand.
Elizabeth Jane Howard, *Something in Disguise*, 1969

In the end there's cruelty and death alone over the land.
Greg Bear, *Eternity*, 1988

---

2 -- Grab the Reader in the First Chapter

Usually the writer's goal is for the first sentence or first paragraph to be the hook. But, as mentioned in chapter 1, the characters have a tendency to take over as they develop.

The characters enjoy taking over more than a sentence.

Some authors create a dynamic first chapter. This chapter's authors describe how they go about using the first chapter as the hook.

Insights

James W. Hall
http://www.jameswhall.com

> **Her memory of that day never lost clarity. Eighteen years later, it was still there, every odor, every word and image, the exact heft of the pistol, each decibel of the explosion detonating again and again in the soft tissues of memory.**

In this opening paragraph of *Body Language* (1998) I try to get the one word theme of the whole novel, as I usually try to do in all my books. In this case, that word repeats twice. Memory. The book is about memory in many ways, the loss of it, the terrifying aspects of a traumatic memory, and there are numerous other aspects of memory at work in the book as well. I usually try to get a one word thematic idea into the opening of my books, not as some kind of literary trick, but so that I will be able to stay on-key throughout the whole book. Of course, in my case, the first words of the novel are usually close to the last words written because I'm not sure of what the book's about till I'm almost done with the first draft.

Stuart Woods
http://www.stuartwoods.com/

Benny Pope stole the boat because he had never been fishing.

The first sentence of *Under the Lake* made something happen fast. It wasn't much, but I hope it engaged the reader's attention right away.

Elaine's, late.

(This short sentence opens several novels so far, *New York Dead, Swimming to Catalina,* and *L.A. Dead.*) This opener would be evocative to anybody who had ever been to Elaine's, and maybe even to anybody who ever heard of the place. Maybe it mystified the rest.

I don't think I've written reader-grabbing first sentences. I try to grab them in the first chapter or two.

Mary Balogh
http://www.marybalogh.com

I normally think of the first chapter as the hook, the pages that will draw the reader in and make it impossible for her to put the book down until she has finished it. And that works well for readers who choose by author or by particular genre. But what about those who browse for something new, who glance at opening sentences and either buy or replace the book on the shelf as a result of that small test of its worth? Then a great opening sentence, one that sets the book apart from all the others on the shelf with it, is invaluable. In romance I aim for one that will cause the reader to do a double take, to be so intrigued or puzzled or shocked or amused or even titillated that she just has to read on a couple of pages to find out what that sentence means. And then, of course, the chapter hook takes over.

Consider these opening sentences of mine:

> **The thunderstorm was entirely to blame; without it, all the problems that developed later just would not have happened; without it she would never in a million years have taken him for a lover.** (*The Notorious Rake*, 1992.)

> **It being not quite the thing to advertise in the London papers for a wife, Anthony Earheart, Marquess of Staunton, eldest son and heir of the Duke of Withingsby, advertised instead for a governess.** (*The Temporary Wife*, 1997)

> **"If you could set before me the plainest, dullest, most ordinary female in London,"** Miles Ripley, Earl of Severn, said, **"or in England, for that matter, I would make her an offer without further ado."** (*The Ideal Wife*, 1991)

Do it passionately or not at all.

Off the Shelf

It never pays to resist arrest.
Harold Q. Masur, *Tall, Dark and Deadly*, 1956

But for the grace of God and an untied shoelace, she would have died with the others that day.
Julie Garwood, *Come the Spring*, 1997

There are some men who enter a woman's life and screw it up forever. Joseph Morelli did this to me—not forever, but periodically.
Janet Evanovich, *One for the Money*, 1994

Somehow, using a combination of pride and terror, she managed to keep her head up and to choke back the nausea.
Nora Roberts, *True Lies*, 1991

The master computer of the planet Harmony was afraid.
Orson Scott Card, *The Memory of Earth*, 1992

Last night I dreamt again of Manderley.
DuMaurier, *Rebecca*

Cassia's eyes slowly fluttered open.
The room was dark and shadowed, lit only by a faint fire burning in the blackened stone hearth. Tiny bits of shattered glass littered the area around her. A chair lay on its side at her feet, on of its slender, spiral-turned legs snapped and splintered. The flickering flames had set eerie shapes dancing across the paneled walls that surrounded her, adding to the already hellish atmosphere of the room.
Jaclyn Reding, *Chasing Dreams,* 1995

It was one of those jobs you take on when things are very lean.
Bill Pronzini, *Undercurrent,* 1973

Remember to smile a lot, John Renfrew thought moodily.
Gregory Benford, *Timescape*, 1980

Estcarp, the last-held land of the Old Ones in the latter days, was ruled by the Witch Women with the Power that had once been the heritage of all those from whom they had sprung.
Andre Norton, *Ware Hawk*, 1983

It was going to be a lousy day. She was sure of that, even before she vanished.
Andrew Klavan, *The Animal Hour*, 1993

Charley Barton was the staff of an East New York establishment that supplied used gas stoves on a wholesale basis.
Avram Davidson, *And Don't Forget the One Red Rose*, 1975

The voluptuous blond woman lifted up on an elbow and pulled a sheet to her breasts.
Judith McNaught, *Something Wonderful*, 1988

"You *can't* marry him!"
Pamela Belle, *The Lode Star*, 1987

His wife had held him in her arms as if she could keep death away from him.
Philip Jose Farmer, *To Your Scattered Bodies Go*, 1971

Insights

Henry G. Stratmann, M.D.

I agree strongly with you about the importance of "hooking" the reader as quickly and firmly as possible with a story's opening sentence or two. Mr. Wolfe's comments on the value of presenting a "disruption of the normal order" is, I think, an excellent point. Several of the stories I've sold to Analog have begun with a variation of that technique—presenting an idea or concept in the first sentence that goes against conventional wisdom. For example, in my novelette "The Best is Yet to Be" (Analog, 12/96), the first sentence is,

"But what if I don't want to live forever?"

Most readers, I think, would like to live forever—so hopefully they'll be interested in finding out why this character doesn't.

Or, "The Human Touch" (Analog, 5/98) begins,

"Congratulations, Mr. Jackson! You've won—a trip to the hospital!"

Not only would the average reader probably think that going to the hospital is hardly something to be congratulated for, but the fact that Mr. Jackson has "won" this dubious privilege will hopefully pique the reader's interest.

Another technique I like is to keep the opening sentence(s) very short and strongly emotional. "The Eumenide" (Analog, 1/98) begins with a character screaming **"Murderer! Baby killer!"** then lunging to attack another character. Alternatively, one can also start with some kind of catastrophic event designed to grab the reader's attention. My novella "Symphony in a Minor Key" (Analog, 10/96) literally begins with a bang:

> **As he emerged from the alley the front of the building on his right exploded.**

Finally, another technique I like to use occasionally is to preface the story proper with a brief quotation reflecting a theme in it. "The Eumenide" starts by quoting from the play "The Eumenides" by Aeschylus:

> **I, the mind of the past, to be driven under the ground out cast, like dirt! The wind I breathe is fury and utter hate.**

Or, "Tempora Mutantur" (a short story about an unexpected hazard of building a time machine, which will be published in Analog in a few months) begins with an English translation of an old epigram originally in Latin:

> **The Times are Chang'd, and in them Chang'd are we./ How? Man, as Times grow worse, grows worse, we see.**

My goal in using these esoteric/enigmatic quotations is to get the reader to frown and ask "What the hell is that supposed to mean, and how's it related to what goes on in the story?"—and, hopefully, be encouraged to read the story and find out.

Carol Dennis
http://www.lar-ryk.com

Dragon's Pawn began:

> **The Keepers met in the vast Hall of the Gate. Twelve pairs of concerned eyes watched Andronan, their silver-haired leader, his long-fingered hands resting quietly on the table before him. the ancient mage said, "We must act now, before it is too late." (1987)**

I believe the hook should set the mood of the story and have an element that hints at conflict to come. Since this story tells of the battle between earthling Jarl Koenig, who doesn't believe in magic, and the Shadowlord, ancient master of magic, the urgency of naming the reluctant Jarl as hero of Realm begins my story.

Dragon's Knight, the second book in the trilogy, began:

> **Four beings of pure energy joined in a preordained meeting, shaping a vast hall from the dust of interstellar space. Then, simply because they had the power to do so, they recreated the forms they had once worn.**
>
> **"The time for vengeance is at hand," Oron, a tall golden plume of light, intoned in the minds of the others.** (1989)

The third book, *Dragon's Queen*, began:

> **Silver moonbeams illuminated the snakelike form as it moved over Lealor's wrist. Its glassy body reflected the moon-blanched colors of the covers. Lealor's red hair fanned dark against her pale features. In the air outside the tower window, a vortex of shadows whirled, then stabilized into the form of a huge dragon.**
> **Wyrd had returned to Realm.**

I like to create hooks that give the reader a visual introduction to the story. This is especially important in fantasy since the reader is entering a whole new world.

Hooks need to introduce the main characters as soon as possible. Here Wyrd discusses the necessity of protecting the heroine Lealor. I was in hopes of luring the reader on by setting a mysterious milieu for the tale.

I think it's only fair to tell you that I have grown as a writer since I penned these beginnings. I think now, I crammed too much backstory in my hooks.

Perhaps you should remind your author readers that they consider how their hook will look to them in future years!

Martha Bayless

The way I see it, openings have two functions: to entice the reader into the world of the book, as Alice was enticed into following the rabbit with the pocket-watch; and to make the entry into that world easy and absorbing -- as easy as Alice tumbling into the rabbit-hole. As a reader, I like to have my bearings in the story by the end of the first paragraph, and at times I do get frustrated by openings that try to mystify me to coax me further into the story. What intrigues me is not what the opening doesn't tell me, but what it does: the three-dimensional clarity of the world sketched in by a few quick lines. (To illustrate this I'm not going to provide examples from my own works -- whether my openings are clear and suspenseful is for readers to decide. All I know is the models I use, and those I will be happy to cite!) Here's a superb example, the end of the opening paragraph of Graham Greene's *The Quiet American*:

> **A lot of old women in black trousers squatted on the landing: it was February and I suppose too hot for them in bed. One trishaw driver pedaled slowly by towards the river-front and I could see lamps burning where they had disembarked the new American planes. There was no sign of Pyle anywhere in the long street.**

Three sentences, and already we know we're in the East (in Vietnam, in fact), at night, in a city with a river, in the heat, with a looming American presence, and that someone named Pyle is ominously missing. (To see the real power of each word, try the final sentence without the word "long" -- something's missing, isn't it?) There's an opening that works for its living, and yet it goes by as easily as Fred Astaire dancing across a stage.

Nowadays novels often begin in the midst of action, because it's a cost-effective way of drawing the reader into the world. Yet I think there's also a place for books that set the scene not in action but in mood. Take this example, the opening of Mrs. Henry Wood's high-Victorian sensationalist novel *Lord Oakburn's Daughters*, where the sense of scandal underlying a repressed society is nicely conveyed by the admirably repressed prose:

A small country town in the heart of England was the scene some few years ago of a sad tragedy. I must ask my readers to bear with me while I relate it. These crimes, having their rise in the evil passions of our nature, are not the most pleasant for the pen to record; but it cannot be denied that they do undoubtedly bear for many of us an interest almost amounting to fascination. I think the following account of what took place will bear such an interest for you.

Even now, the used-bookstores can't keep Mrs. Henry Wood on the shelves: the novels sell out as soon as they come in. There's a lot to be said for the short sharp opening, but there's also something to be said for the slow boil.

Off the Shelf

One things about boundary lines, Curtis Daniels thought, as he twisted a little in his saddle in an attempt to ease his aching back, they didn't mean a whole hell of a lot when it came to the weather.
L.J. Washburn, *Riders of the Monte*, 1990

At dawn, if it was low tide on the flats, I would awaken to the chatter of gulls.
Norman Mailer, *Tough Guys Don't Dance*, 1984

Every time they got a call from the leper hospital to pick up a body Jack Delaney would feel himself coming down with the flu or something.
Elmore Leonard, *Bandits*, 1987

"This is some mess in here," Monoghan said.
Ed McBain, *Poison*, 1987

I shouldn't have taken either case.
Linda Barnes, *The Snake Tattoo*, 1989

Sitting on the hood and thrumming the strings of his chevycap, Aldo watched the sun rise over the black semi in the slow lane.
Gene Wolfe, *Bluesberry Jam*, 1996

The room was still empty.
Tom Clancy, *Clear and Present Danger*, 1989

"Everybody should fear only one person, and that person should be himself."
Philip Jose Farmer, *The Magic Labrinth*, 1980

You better not never tell nobody but God.
Alice Walker, *The Color Purple*, 1982

"She must be stopped from coming here."
Phyllis A. Whitney, *Amethyst Dreams*, 1997

Kate knew she was going to be famous. She just didn't know what for.
Pat Booth, *American ICON*, 1998

Freak accidents ran in the family.
Karen Karbo, *The Diamond Lane*, 1991

Nicholas was trying to concentrate on the letter to his mother, a letter that was probably the most important document he would ever write.
Jude Deveraux, *A Knight in Shining Armor*, 1989

Everyone now knows how to find the meaning of life within himself.
Kurt Vonnegut, *The Sirens of Titan*, 1959

Folks from back East look at you funny when you talk about that sense that tells you when someone is aiming to put a bullet in your back.
Bill Pinnell, *Terror on the Border*, 1991

Cullom rode out of a canyon blackness that was like a massive weight pressing against him on both sides and into a lingering purple dusk.
Carter Travis Young, *Blaine's Law*, 1974

As I grew out of childhood it began to dawn on me that there was something rather mysterious about my presence in the Silk House.
Victoria Holt, *Silk Vendetta*, 1987

My name is Prince Ivan the Simple, and I am the son of Prince Ivan the Bold.
Gene Wolfe, *The Death of Koshchei the Deathless*, 1995

The giant knew Richard Nixon.
Jonathan Kellerman, *Monster*, 1999

The child lay still; anyone observing it would have been certain it was sound asleep.
John Saul, *Nightshade*, 2000

Jane Yolen
http://www.janeyolen.com/

This is from an essay of mine:

Call me Ishmael.

That is considered one of the world's greatest opening lines. It starts with a mystery: not "My name is Ishmael." Or "The fellows call me Ishmael." But a request, or perhaps an order, that the narrator shall be known henceforth as Ishmael. An odd name that, but for a nineteenth century readership, one that immediately recalls the Biblical Ishmael--the child driven into the wilderness with his slave mother. The unwanted, forgotten, once beloved child who threatens a dynasty. The forsaken hero. The dark brother. The other side of the Semitic coin.

Justin Leiber

I began the second novel of my "Beyond" trilogy, *Beyond Humanity*, with a quote from the diary of a man who concurrently commanded the entire British navy:

By and by we are called to Sir W. Battens to see the strange creature that Captain Holmes hath brought with him from Guiny; it is a great baboone, but so much like a man in most things, that (although they say there is a Species of them) yet I cannot believe but that it is a monster got of a man and a she-baboone: I do believe

it already understands much English; and I am of the mind that it might be taught to speak or make signs. -- Diary of Samuel Pepys, 24 August 1661.

The Secretary of the Admiralty is a marvelous prophet and man of uncommon sense. Though the matter is still in scientific debate, the last few decades of primate research have indeed established that great apes can understand some spoken English and can be "taught" to "make signs," though, with their limited vocal apparatus, they cannot mimic spoken language. Even Pepys' speculation that humans and apes can produce offspring has some confirmation in the case of the chimpanzee (chimpanzees and humans share 98% of their genes, more than donkeys and horses for example). This passage prefigures where *Beyond Humanity* will go (including the lurid possibility I just mentioned) but it also anchors the novel in historical fact.

Your request for "what fiction experts say about their opening sentences," along with Gene Wolfe's example of a single opening sentence, send me scurrying through each opening sentence of my four other novels and an equal number of my other books. I didn't find any opening sentence that was up to the Pepys' standard. I attribute this to the shortness of my sentences. You need a whole number of them to mount up to the complexity of Pepys' sentence. Our century's popular fiction has thrown out the semi-colons, colons, and parens that decorated seventeenth century prose. Replaced them with periods. No wonder the sentences are short.

I did, however, find something promisingly long in the opening of a paper I gave to an academic conference on "Intertextualities." The motto for this paper comes from that old invertionizer Oscar Wilde: "Nature imitates Art."

Considering the present aggressive stance of literary theorists, detonating, denuding, and deconstructing the humble scrivener's offerings as if works of fiction were the shoulders of midgets on which the giants of critical theory may grind their jackboots, you will think me rash to confess to the jejune offense of novel writing, but I mean not only to confess but also to explain and justify--even, indeed, to revel--in the

inversion of fiction and life that is our lot, revel, that is, in an inversion both more enduring and more significant than that between fiction and literary theory.

English Department literary prose exists on the edge of self-parody. Easy, though, when you get the hang of it. As a philosopher masquerading as an English Professor, it took me the plane ride from Houston to Tallahassee to write the paper. Somewhere over the Mississippi I discovered I was Shakespeare. Altitude and the mushroom in my martini.

Shirley Rousseau Murphy
http://www.joegrey.com

Regarding the Joe Grey mysteries: My first sentence is never a complete hook to the story, it's a hook to the opening paragraph. It takes a paragraph to set the scene as I want, to create a sense of place for the reader and make him comfortable, and to introduce my cat-on-the-scene. But hey, these are cozies; we can take a little time here.

Cat on the Edge:

The murder of Samuel Beckwhite in the alley behind Jolly's Delicatessen was observed by no human witness.

This is not a complete hook without the next sentence:

Only the grey tomcat saw Beckwhite fall, the big man's heavy body crumpling, his round, close-trimmed head crushed from the blow of a shiny steel wrench.

The last sentence in the paragraph completes the action:

At the bright swing of the weapon and the thud of breaking bone, the cat stiffened with alarm and backed deeper into the shadows, a sleek silver ripple in the dark.

Again in *Cat Under Fire*, I rely on the first two sentences to set up the story:

> **The night was cool, and above the village hills the stars hurled down their ancient light-born messages. High up on the open slopes where the grass blew tall and rank, a small hunter crouched hidden, his ears and whiskers flat to his sleek head, his yellow eyes burning.**

This leads into one of my favorite—and graphically bloody—hunting scenes.

> **The chronological point of murder, in the book, affects the immediacy of the opening: EDGE opens with the murder. In FIRE, the murder has already happened—so I take a little time to hunt mice, and introduce the murder gradually.**

In *Cat Raise the Dead*, we are not aware of any death until well into the book. Again I lay the scene more slowly, painting the windy night and the predatory tomcat stalking an unknown woman. The first sentence hints at the tension:

> **Within the dark laundry room she stood to the side of the door's narrow glass, where she would not be seen from the street, stood looking out into the night.**

Nor does *Cat in the Dark* begin with death but with the setting of place:

> **The cat crouched in darkness beneath the library desk, her tabby stripes mingled with the shadows, her green eyes flashing light, her tail switching impatiently as she watched the last patrons linger around the circulation desk.**

Cat to the Dogs does begin with a murder; but it did not satisfy me to kill the driver and hurl his car over the cliff all in the first sentence:

In the depths of Hellhag Canyon the fog hung so thick Joe Grey couldn't see his paws, mist as heavy as cream clinging to the bushes and rocks, the invisible branches of willow scrub telegraphing through his whiskers as sharp as electrical charges—no sound but the hushing of the sea until suddenly from the road above, the screaming of tires as a lone car skidded, crashed against boulders and flipped over the edge, thundering as it fell straight toward him battering against the mountain: he streaked away, was jolted nearly out of his hide as the car landed inches from him, shaking the ravine like another California quake.

I hurled the car, yes. But I left Joe Grey to discover the fact of murder at a cat's slower, inquisitive pace. And as to whether the first paragraph of *Cat to the Dogs* will remain as one sentence, I really can't say. The book is at present in rough draft; it's the final form will follow, like Joe Grey himself, where the mood leads.

Off the Shelf

The catastrophic love affair characterized by sexual obsession has been a professional interest of mine for many years now.
Patrick McGrath, *Asylum*, 1997

It was beginning to feel like the year it rained twice.
Judith Van Gieson, *Hotshots*, 1996

In the moments before the brutal murder of Jack Novak ended what she later thought of as her time of innocence, Assistant County Prosecutor Stella Marz gazed down at the waterfront of her native city, Steelton.
Richard North Patterson, *Dark Lady*, 1999

After nearly a quarter of a century of marriage, Richie Meyers, my husband, told me to call him Rick. Then he started slicking back his hair with thirty-five-dollar-a-jar English pomade.
Susan Isaacs, *After All These Years*, 1993

Dexter Whitlaw carefully sealed the box, securing every seam with a roll of masking tape he had stolen from Wal-Mart the day before.
Linda Howard, *Kill and Tell*, 1998

"Have you reached a verdict?" Judge Alfred Neff asked the eight men and four women seated in the jury box.
Phillip Margolin, *Gone, But Not Forgotten*, 1993

Brown butcher's paper, crisp edges folded with a soldier's precision, an address in block letters. Blue ink. Someone pressed down hard. The parcel was no bigger than a comic book.
Joshua Quittner and Michelle Slatalla, *Flame War*, 1997

The giant knew Richard Nixon.
Jonathan Kellerman, *Monster*, 1999

He should never have taken that shortcut.
Michael Crichton, *Timeline*, 1999

"Vomit," Jansen said, "any splash—blood, excrement, anything like that—dry now mos' likely—just spray it."
Patrick Lynch, *Carriers*, 1995

The sky was an ominous pewter color by the time Police Chief Mitch Bushyhead reached the station.
Jean Hager, *Masked Dancers*, 1998

The various and arcane means by which one human being sometimes ended the life of another had always fascinated Grace Harris, head of the district attorney's homicide trials team, but this one, she thought, took the cake.
John Martel, *The Alternate*, 1999

For three weeks the young killer actually lived in the walls of an extraordinary 15-room beach house.
James Patterson, *Kiss the Girls*, 1995

There is a special clarity of thought, an unclouded focus which is granted to those who shed all fear and panic, who in the end stare death in the eye, and leave this world on their own terms.
Steve Martini, *Undue Influence*, 1994

There's no accounting for laws.
James Crumley, *The Wrong Case*, 1975

Two days after the murder, listening to Brett Allen's tale of innocence and confusion, the lawyer wavered between disbelief and wonder at its richness, so vivid that she could almost picture it as truth.
Richard North Patterson, *The Final Judgment*, 1995

Beneath his attic room, the house slept.
Joan Hall Hovey, *Listen to the Shadows*, 1991

It was a fine night for strolling, but Gabriella Constante hurried.
Lillian O'Donnell, *Dial 577 R-A-P-E*, 1974

Pseudonyms

**"What's the use of their having names," the Gnat said,
"if they won't answer to them?"**
Lewis Carroll, *Through the Looking Glass*, 1872

- Many authors have used the pseudonym Nicholas Carter, but Frederick Van Rensselaer Dey wrote the most prose in that name.

- Floating or house names are often used to hide the fact that one author contributed several articles for a given magazine issue. Two house names are Ivar Jorgensen and Brett Sterling.

- **Some pseudonyms have pseudonyms!** George Sanders and Gypsy Rose Lee were pen names of Craig Rice, whose name was Georgianna Ann Randolph [who happened to be Mrs. Laurence Lipton].

Rejections

- John Creasey wrote 564 books under his 13 pseudonyms. He received over 700 rejection letters before a publisher accepted one of his novels.

- Pearl S. Buck's *The Good Earth* received twelve rejections.

- James Joyce snared over twenty rejections on *Dubliners*.

3 – Techniques to Hook the Reader

The authors in this chapter open a story in many ways, such as using action or a character's thoughts, a romance, a shocking scene, or some conflict. They may introduce the main character or wait until a bit later to bring that one in. They often balance plot and character, while challenging the reader to focus on the conflict.

The first commandment of any writing class is "Show don't tell:" **The woman at the wheel drove over the bumpy path with kids' legs or dog limbs hanging out of every window.** How much better than "The woman had a lot of kids and dogs in her car."

Now see how these writers start the show and keep it going.

Insights

Laurence Shames

The best openings are not the cute ones or the flamboyant ones, but the ones that seem inevitable. Of course the story would start that way...

By this criterion, my favorite lead remains the one from *Florida Straits*:

People go to Key West for lots of different reasons.
Joey Goldman went there to be a gangster.

These two simple sentences set up the whole book. We know that Key West itself will be an important character. We're curious about the other reasons people go there. And we're instantly aware of the improbability of Joey's scheme.

I should stress that I jotted down these sentences simply to get myself started; I thought I'd go back later and do something flashier. Only afterward did I realize that the simplest and most direct way to get myself moving was also the surest and most economical way to get the reader involved.

Joanne Pence
http://members.aol.com/jopence

This is the opening to *Cooking Up Trouble*:

"I wouldn't feed this swill to my cat!" Martin Bayman announced. Angelina Amalfi watched the older, gray-haired man stand, throw his napkin on his plate, and storm from Hill Haven Inn's dining room. The lentil-soybean cutlets were not a hit.

Angie had to agree with Bayman. The cats she knew would have tried to bury them.

I write the Angie Amalfi mystery series. It's a light-hearted, fun series in which I attempt to combine elements of mystery/suspense with humor, a touch of romance, and food. In the opening to *Cooking Up Trouble*, I've attempted to give the flavor (so to speak) of the book and the series. I've let the reader meet Angie, and see that she has an understated, somewhat wry sense of humor. I've also introduced food--in this case some horrible lentil-soybean cutlets. Don't they sound wretched? If you agree, and if you enjoy Angie's take on what's going on, I believe you would continue reading. And that's the whole point.

Sasha Miller
http://www.sff.net/people/sasha

We all know the truism about starting your story at the point that everything changes. This is about the opening, which is different. The opening for your novel or novelette or novella or short story is, literally, the door.

So, to go with this analogy, take a look at the door to the work you're currently laboring over, wondering how on earth to get it started properly. First thing to ask yourself is, Is the door open? Or is it locked with off-putting things like indefinite pronouns, unattributed speech, pseudo action that has no apparent cause.

> **"Oh, drat," he said as he peevishly kicked the dog and set fire to the wastebasket.**

That kind of opening has its own invitation, all right, but it's to depart at all reasonable speed, never to return. Instead, if this is the story you are trying to tell, try something like this:

> **Stanley regarded Fauntleroy the poodle with a jaundiced eye. This was the third time in one week the wretched beast had used the wastebasket as a relief station, rather than the neighbor's yard as any proper dog should do. "Nothing for t," Stanley said resignedly. He struck a match. After three such episodes, that wastebasket had to burn.**

Granted, it's not much of a story at this point, but it does invite the reader to wonder why on earth Stanley couldn't get the leash on Fauntleroy and usher him out the door now and then. And with such mild curiosity going for you, at least some readers will be inclined to read on and find out why.

Therefore, if you are having problems with your openings, my best suggestion is to take a look at that door and see if the mat is brushed and tidy, flanking decorative shrubbery trimmed, fresh paint applied, the old newspapers and other rubble cleared away, and the latch invitingly ajar. It might work wonders.

Russell James
http://dspace.dial.pipex.com/found/rj.htm

The first words are the most important you will write. Most readers don't know who the hell you are and why they should bother with your book. They'll skim through the pages--and there's not much you can do about that, apart from keeping the paragraphs short and not going too far without dialogue--then they'll turn to page one and read your first few words.

And decide whether to stay with you or not.

The first book I had published (note the careful evasion there) was *Underground* --a tale in the 1980s "brutalist" style, but with a tender heart. It began:

> **"You know what I mean? You haven't seen him, but the hairs on the back of your neck tickle against your collar. It makes you shiver. Everything looks normal but it ain't. It's like you got a belly-dancer sucking Turkish delight while she blows hot breath down the back of your neck. You don't mistake that."**

I used that deliberately off-the-wall image to set against the hard-boiled style and tell the reader that this book was amusing and not just a tough guy rant.

In *Daylight*, I wanted the tough hero (who also reveals a far softer side later) to get his grievance across first. The book started:

> **The guy driving the car is called Louis. He was in Pentonville with me. He was serving three years for aggravated burglary and didn't get parole. So we had two years together.**
>
> **I didn't get parole either. Sentences of five years or over usually don't. Especially if the offence involves drugs or violence.**
>
> **When they added my sentences together, there was a total of eight years. Prisoners get a third off anyway, whatever we do, so that gave me five years four**

months, before parole. With parole I could have come out in under three years. But I didn't. I could have come out in under four. But I didn't.

Those early books were told in the first person. When I switched to third person I wanted to keep the immediacy. The opening of *Slaughter Music* suggested that the book was going to be another first person story, but it wasn't. I used the chatty opening to draw readers in:

That's the one: that house half-hidden through a tangle of trees and shrubbery behind a wall. Not as difficult as it looks. High brick wall; jagged glass at the top. Looks vicious, doesn't it? That's some wall - it has been there a while. But weather has softened the edges of those broken glass teeth: wind and rain, snow settling. The sharpness has gone. D'you remember how it feels when you pick up a piece of bottle glass from the beach - all the edges worn down? Well, on top of that old wall there, the glass will be like that. Won't hurt you at all."

John Legg
http://members.aol.com/JackBooks/homepage1.html

Ezra Early knelt next to the thing — it was the only way he could describe it, since it was no longer a human being — lying on the desolate stretch of Cimarron desert.

While I often go for an action opening, this somewhat static, but quite powerful opening popped into my head for a book titled *Southwest Thunder*. I think its raw potency really grabs the reader, shocking them into wanting to find out what this "thing" is, and once they find out, they'll want to what happens to the perpetrators.

I did a series called *Saddle Tramp* for Berkley (under the pen name Clint Hawkins). The main character, Wade Calhoun, was one tough hombre. And we wanted to start the series with something of a bang. This is what I came up with:

> **Wade Calhoun felt a jolt of satisfaction as the blade of his Bowie knife bit deep into his foe's ample supply of belly flesh and then chunked off the breastbone.**

This introduces Calhoun in a grand fashion. It shows that he is not a man to be fooled with, and I think pulls readers into the story. Why is our "hero" gutting this guy like a fish? I think the reader understands implicitly that while Calhoun is a hard man and as tough as they come, that he must have a reason for doing something like this. So they will read on to find out.

One thing I did with Calhoun was to find a different way with each novel to kill off his horse. Sometimes they were funny, sometimes not. But one time — in *Sioux Trail*, No. 6 in the series — I used that to open the book:

> **Wade Calhoun's bony old horse just sort of keeled over and died, with one last flurry of flatulent grandeur.**

Here's a case of grabbing the reader with humor that fits right in with the series, and is something of a counterpoint to the character. Calhoun is generally a dour kind of guy, and with humor like this, I think it really sets a different scene for him, while at the same time is still compelling for the reader. By this time, the reader, who is likely to be a fan of the series, knows about Calhoun and his horses, and will want to know just what *this* one is all about.

My openings, like most of my ideas for novels and most of my writing, are almost instinctive. These things just come to me somehow. It is, in some ways, rather eerie. Not that I don't put thought into them. It's more like I just kind of let my mind roll it around for a while, and the answer pops out. It is a strange process, but a wonderful gift, I guess you could call it.

Paul Levinson
http://www.sfwa.org/members/levinson

> **Jeff felt a certain hardness under his backside, like he had fallen asleep on a plush chair and come awake on a park bench somewhere.**

He opened his eyes and stared at his destiny.

Those opening lines from my 1997 novella, "Loose Ends" (published in Analog, nominated for the Hugo, Nebula, and Sturgeon Awards), are among my favorites.

They say nothing about the character or the place he is in, except he somehow does not belong there. They are definite about just one thing: he is a man in some kind of flux, a traveler. The opener is, in other words, clearly ambiguous -- which means that it invites the reader to find more...

In Marshall McLuhan's terms, ambiguous stimuli are "cool," and invite participation to fill in their gaps. At whom are those eyes behind the sunglasses looking? If we can present just enough information to whet the reader's appetite -- not enough to satiate, just to whet -- then the reader is most likely to become our partner as we make our way through the story that ensues. Or, as Stephane Mallarme said, "to define is to kill, to suggest is to create..."

Off the Shelf

Claire won the lottery on a Wednesday afternoon in May, the same afternoon that Emma graduated from high school, the dog ran away, and the landlord raised the rent.
Judith Michael, *Pot of Gold*, 1993

You can't be happy in this life because of what happened in your past lives.
Jude Deveraux, *Remembrance*, 1994

Someone was watching her.
Catherine Coulter, *The Cove*, 1996

There were 117 psychoanalysts on the Pan Am flight to Vienna and I'd been treated by at least six of them.
Erica Jong, *Fear of Flying*, 1973

I never was a virgin.
Susan Isaacs, *Lily White*, 1996

In his senior year at college Hamilton Mack was voted "the man whose personality was most likely to split."
Harold Q. Masur, *Make a Killing*, 1964

Once upon a time when the world was young there was a Martian named Smith.
Robert Heinlein, *Stranger in a Strange Land*, 1961

Jinn and Phyllis were spending a wonderful holiday in space, as far away as possible from the inhabited stars.
Pierre Boulle, *Planet of the Apes*, 1963

You'd think a fellow would learn to take his own advice.
Frank Roderus, *Charlie and the Sir*, 1988

It is said we have ten seconds when we wake of a morning, to remember what it was we dreamed the night before.
Richard Bach, *A Gift of Wings*, 1974

The alarm went off at six; Dutheil got up at quarter past, obeying movements long since formalized into a ritual.
Nicholas Freeling, *This is the Castle*, 1968

By the time he graduated from college John Smith had forgotten all about the bad fall he took on the ice that January day in 1953.
Stephen King, *The Dead Zone*, 1979

When I was a little girl I used to dress Barbie up without underpants.
Janet Evanovich, *High Five*, 1999

"God, I want this maniac!"
Nancy Taylor Rosenberg, *Buried Evidence*, 2000

Women never use their intelligence--
except when they need to prop up their intuition.
Jacques Deval, News summaries, 1954

Insights

Anne McCaffrey

About reader hooks...well, they come with the story I'm trying to tell, so it's no good giving examples - except perhaps the first lines of my own books - Like

Lessa woke, cold.

Okay, where did she wake? Why was she cold? Does she warm up? Does her situation improve? Disimprove? Who is she?

I certainly don't have any formula - except a line that will make the reader want to know what's going to happen in this story.

Nancy Kress

http://srd.yahoo.com/srst/8306095/author+nancy+kress/1/1/*http://www.sff.net/people/nankr
ess/

An opening sentence needs to do a number of things. It should raise questions in the reader's mind—questions that he or she will then keep reading to get answered. It should indicate the voice of the work: ironic, heroic, wry, mimetic, cynical. And it should at least begin to orient us in space and time. The following sentences from my work attempt to meet these criteria in various ways.

**The first day of school, we had assault-with-intent in
Ms. Kelly's room.** *Fault Lines*

Here the opening tone is slightly ironic. This comes from the contrast of such evocations of childhood as "first day of school" and "Ms. Kelly's room" with the legal jargon of "assault-with-intent." The pronoun "we" indicates a personal involvement on the part of the narrator. Questions are raised to interest the reader: Why was the assault committed? What was the outcome? Finally, we are given a setting: a school, probably (again, from the legal term) in the late twentieth century.

> **When I finally found God, he was slumped at the counter in a Detroit diner, stirring his coffee.** *Grant Us This Day*

Here the tone is both fantastic and wry: God reduced to a corporeal being in a slump at a diner. Questions are raised: Why is He in a slump? Who is the narrator, and why is he looking for God? We also get a definite setting, unexpected to the subject matter: a diner in Detroit.

> **They sat stiffly on his antique Eames chairs, two People who didn't want to be here, or one who didn't want to and one who resented the other's reluctance.** *Beggars in Spain*

Here, too, questions are suggested: Why is one person reluctant to be here and one not? Where is "here"? The tone is straightforward, reportorial, which does in fact foreshadow the way the rest of the novel will be written. Finally, the phrase "antique Eames chairs" suggests to the discerning that this is the future, since furniture is not rated as "antique" until it is at least one hundred years old, and Eames introduced his famous chairs in the 1950's.

Off the Shelf

Most days, I'm all right.
Bill Pronzini, *Jackpot*, 1990

It was raining when they rolled me out of the big Lincoln and into the ditch.
Earl W. Emerson, *Yellow Dog Party*, 1991

"A pickle may not remember getting pickled, but that doesn't make it a cucumber."
Linda Barnes, *Coyote*, 1991

My lover came to me on the last night in April with a message and a warning that sent me home to him.
Mary Stewart, *Touch Not the Cat*, 1976

I feel compelled to report that at the moment of death, my entire life did not pass before my eyes in a flash.
Sue Grafton, *"I" is for Innocent*, 1992

Years ago, in state documents, Vachel Carmouche was always referred to as the electrician, never as the executioner.
James Lee Burke, *Purple Cane Road*, 2000

"What the devil am I to do!"
Barbara Cartland, *The Daring Deception*, 1973

A therapist's work is never over.
Jonathan Kellerman, *Private Eyes*, 1992

Pippin looked out from the shelter of Gandalf's cloak.
J.R.R. Tolkien, *The Return of the King*, 1956

From the broom closet, Consuela could head the two American ladies arguing in Room 404.
Margaret Millar, *The Listening Walls*, 1959

It was several hours since the news of his wife's death had reached him and it still seemed unbelievable, it still had the power to shock.
Constance Heaven, *The Queen and the Gypsy*, 1977

Multi-Genre Authors

Below are some authors who don't limit their work to one genre.

Author	Mystery	SF	Western	Romance
Margery Allingham	X	X		
Poul Anderson		X	X	
Anthony Boucher	X	X		
Alfred Coppel	X	X		
John Creasey	X	X	X	X
Stanley Ellin	X	X		
S.A. Lombino	X	X		
John D. MacDonald	X	X		
Sax Rohmer	X	X		
Robert Silverberg	X	X		
Loren Estleman		X	X	
Elmore Leonard		X	X	
Bill Pronzini	X		X	

Courtni Wright

http://srd.yahoo.com/goo/author+courtni+wright/1/*http://www.erols.com/courtni/

> **I can do this, Jenna thought, looking straight ahead.
> I'm ready. Nothing will stop me now. I'm beginning a
> new day and a new life. This is one more crossing and
> one more chance to grow. I'm ready.** (*It Had To Be You*)

I sometimes use a character's thoughts to open the first chapter in order to show the reader the conflict that will unfold during the novel. In this case, the heroine has overcome many obstacles to success and risen from her humble roots to a coveted position in a respected law office.

On this her first day, she doubts her ability to compete and must give herself a pep talk with every step that takes her closer to the goal for which she has worked so diligently. Hopefully, by encouraging the reader to see inside the character's mind and feel the turmoil of her emotions, the actions of the plot will unfold in a manner that will engage the reader immediately and keep the interest alive.

Nina Gettler w/a Nina Beaumont

As a writer who loves narrative and exposition, I haven't been very clever at writing a first sentence that hooks the reader. The one exception is in my book *Surrender the Heart*, where the first line belongs to the heroine's mother who says,

> **"Ariane, if you don't take that bored look off her face, you're never going to get a husband."**

I was rather proud of that first line because it summarized the basic premise of the story--a heroine who was supposed to catch a husband and had no interest in doing so.

John Paxton Sheriff

Aspiring writers are constantly told to start their novels or short stories with a bang; to grab their readers by the throat from the outset, and never let go. Good advice, surely, for the very best openings not only force the reader to read on by posing a question, they also - in few words – establish the setting and hint at the mood.

> **Marshal Frank Seeger brought the bad news from Deep Bend to the Keen spread at Middle Creek, riding in with his long frame hunched inside a shiny yellow slicker as the first ice-cold splatters of rain blew in from the east.**

The question implicit in that extract from *Bury Him Deep, In Tombstone* is, what bad news? - and to find out, readers will certainly read on. The question all aspiring writers ask is, if the instruction to grab the reader by the throat from the outset is good advice, why then do they see so many books published that don't seem to do that?

The answer, of course, is that they do - but in a less obvious way.

Readers will be drawn into a book by good writing as much as they will by strong fingers clutching at their neck. Compulsive readers like the shape of words as much as their meaning; they will read a well constructed passage as much for its form as for its message - and they will want more. So the soundest advice is not necessarily to grab readers by the throat, but to write at your very best, from the beginning.

The following leisurely opening lines from *The Man From the Staked Plains* establish the setting and hint at the mood, but although the question posed is much more subtle, the urge to read on is, in my opinion, just as strong.

> **With the arrival of spring it was his habit to step outside the old cabin when the sun was still a cold light beyond the horizon. After a night swathed in rough blankets he relished the feel of the chill breeze on his bare chest, the wash of clear, pine-scented air through lungs that were clogged and stale after hours of sleep in the single, shuttered room; the intensity of the light after dreaming restlessly of haunting shadows.**

Sara Hoskinson Frommer
http://www.sff.net/people/SaraHoskinsonFrommer/index.htp

The murder in *Murder in C Major* takes a while to arrive, but I didn't want my readers to wonder whether there would be one. So I lifted a thought from a later chapter for that first sentence. Though when the reader finally comes on Joan ironing, nothing turns out to be quite the way that first sentence seems.

> **Ironing for a corpse wasn't Joan Spencer's idea of fun.**

(The first sentence) also proves the value of self-editing. My first draft began,

> **"Ironing for a corpse had never been part of Joan Spencer's mental job description for a mother working her son's way through college."**

Terry Brooks
www.randomhouse.com/delrey

The following sentence opens *Running with the Demon*, published as a first edition hardcover by Ballantine Books in September, 1997:

He stands alone in the center of another of America's burned-out towns, but he has been to this one before.

I like this sentence because it tells you something important about the story right away—it isn't happening in the present. The suggestion of a scorched earth landscape is decidedly futuristic. It might be the Armageddon we all fear, but assuredly some sort of war has occurred. The unknown protagonist is traveling this ravaged landscape, one town to the next, for reasons as yet unrevealed. Something about this particular town is special, though, because he apparently hasn't visited the others more than once.

Finally, this sentence and the ones that follow are italicized, which suggests that what we are reading is set outside the normal flow of the story. This is a written account, a memory or a dream.

The trick to writing a good first sentence is to raise enough questions about what's happening that the reader will have to turn the pages to find out.

Off the Shelf

Sleeping fitfully, a big man bulging out of T-shirt and shorts, I wander through a dream where I'm a stranger seeking some palpable reality, a cry on my lips: Where the hell am I?
Andrew Coburn, *The Trespassers*, 1974

Customs of courtship vary greatly in different times and places, but the way the thing happens to be done here and now always seems the only natural way to do it.
Herman Wouk, *Marjorie Morningstar*, 1955

It was love at first sight.
Joseph Heller, *Catch-22*, 1955

At eight in the morning of his last day in Boston, Sean Burke paced out tight circles on the corner of Kenmore Square, waiting for the abortionist, a nine-millimeter semiautomatic handgun hidden in the inside pocket of his army jacket.
Richard North Patterson, *No Safe Place*, 1998

Detective Steve Carella wasn't sure he had heard the man correctly.
Ed McBain, *Sadie When She Died*, 1972

By the time they had lived seven years in the little house on Greentree Avenue in Westport, Connecticut, they both detested it.
Sloan Wilson, *The Man in the Gray Flannel Suit*, 1955

It took Christy precisely five weeks to achieve her objectives.
Juliette Mead, *Intimate Strangers*, 1996

The man at the safe worked swiftly but without haste.
John Creasey, *The Baron in France*, 1953

He sat perfectly still in front of the television set in room 932 of the Biltmore Hotel.
Mary Higgins Clark, *A Stranger is Watching*, 1977

I am writing this book because I understand that "revelations" are soon to appear about that great man who was once my husband, attacking his character, and my own.
Joyce Cary, *Prisoner of Grace*, 1952

If you really want to hear about it, the first thing you'll probably want to know is where I was born, and what my lousy childhood was like, and how my parents were occupied and all before they had me, and all that David Copperfield kind of crap, but I don't feel like going into it, if you want to know the truth.
J.D. Salinger, *Catcher in the Rye*, 1951

When this nameless piece a' shit tore off Linda Lobo's G-string instead of sticking money in it like he was supposed to, Texas Jack Carmine went crazy-over-the-edge and hit him with a pool cue.
Robert James Waller, *Border Music*, 1995

The American handed Leamus another cup of coffee and said, "Why don't you go back to sleep? We can ring you if he shows up."
John LeCarre, *The Spy Who Came in From the Cold*, 1963

The sky above the port was the color of television, tuned to a dead channel.
William Gibson, *Neuromancer*, 1984

I am too young to die.
Harry Harrison, *The Stainless Steel Rat Gets Drafted*, 1987

David Ogden took a long time to die, and he did not die unnoticed.
Herbert Buckholz, *Brain Damage*, 1992

Misery, Mary thought.
David Rabe, *The Crossing Guard*, 1995

"I don't believe it, of course," said Golan Tervize, standing on the wide steps of Seldon Hall and looking out over the city as it sparkled in the sunlight.
Isaac Asimov, *Foundations' Edge*, 1982

"I am innocent," George Ives said confidently.
Ralph Compton, *The Virginia City Trail*, 1994

Cursing the inventors of pantyhose, June weddings, and Southern tradition, Skip took the arm of the freckle-faced young usher and walked down the damn aisle.
Julie Smith, *A Match Made in Hell*

The editor of the Domingo Weekly Observer leaned against the doorjamb and chewed impatiently on an unlighted cigar as he frowned at the lazy street.
Elmer Kelton, *Manhunters*, 1974

Collaborative Teams:
Mystery & Science Fiction Pseudonyms

Pseudonym	Authors
Emma Lathen	Mary J. Latis & Martha Hennissart
Wade Miller	Bob Wade & Bill Miller
Robert Randall	Robert Silverberg & Randall Garrett
Ellery Queen	Frederic Dannay & Manfred B. Lee
Peter Antony	Peter and Anthony Shaffer
S.D. Gottesman	Cyril Kornbluth, Frederik Pohl, & Robert Lowndes
Manning Coles	Cyril Henry Coles & Adelaide Manning
Paul Dennis Lavond	Cyril Kornbluth, Frederik Pohl, & Robert Lowndes
Scott Mariner	Cyril M. Kornbluth & Frederik Pohl
Kelley Roos	Audrey Kelley & William Roos

Cats in the Pages

Cats live in the pages of many women mystery writers, including Doug Allyn, Linda Barnes, Christianna Brand, Lilian Braun, Jon L. Breen, Patricia Cornwell, Bill Crider, Peter Crowther, Debbie De Louise, Carole Nelson Douglas, Carol Gorman, Sue Grafton, Patricia Highsmith, Bentley Little, Patricia Moyes, Bruce Holland Rogers, Dell Shannon, Mary Stewart, and Pauline Glen Winslow.

I can find women who have never had one love affair, but it is rare indeed to find any who have had only one.
Francois Alexandre Frederic Duc De LaRochefoucauld-Liancourt , *Maxims*, n.d. (1747-1827)

4 -- Do Hooks Matter?

We established the need for conflict in chapter 1. In this chapter we tear that apart by adding conflict on conflict.

Here we cover the authors who show the full range of views towards the hook. Some authors insist a hook is an unnecessary opening. This chapter presents these opposing opinions as well as the hook die hards.

Thus, for new writers who struggle with the weight of those first sentences, this chapter can be a refreshing counterpoint.

Insights

Michael Connelly
http://www.michaelconnelly.com/

Opening lines do not mean that much to me. I don't follow any kind of philosophy about hooking people with a first line or paragraph. Subsequently, maybe my opening lines are boring, but there is something that doesn't sit right with me about needing a hook in the very first line in order to get someone to read a 400-page book. Yet there are many, many writers who think the opposite of me. That makes your subject a worthy one.

Loren D. Estleman
www.lorenestleman.com

First sentences are extremely important to me. All told, I think I put more effort into this "best foot forward" than into any other part of the book. My personal favorite, from *Bloody Season*:

He was dying faster than usual that morning, striping the sides of the dry-sink with bloody sputum and shreds of shattered lung.

Joan Van Nuys
http://www.eclectics.com/joan/index.html

Editor's note: I was shocked to learn of this author's sudden death May 20, 2000. I am forever grateful that she shared with us her thoughts-- some of the last printed paragraphs of Joan Van Nuys.

When Shara asked me to comment on the importance of having a compelling first sentence in a book, my mind went blank. We all know you need a hook in the beginning to draw the reader in. The rule is written in gold at the top of every how-to list on bookwriting. But had I followed it? I couldn't remember.

I got my books out, checked the first one, checked the second and felt the floor yawning open beneath me. Unbelievable. There was no hook in either one. What in heaven's name was I thinking and why hadn't my editor and agent caught it? I have no answer except the obvious one. Maybe not every book needs a hook.

My other books have them and it's clear they're needed to set the mood and introduce the story:

Ian's heart felt heavy as he left Cavanaugh Hall. (*Forever Beloved, 1996*)

Pain awakened Ben from his long sleep. (*Beloved Deceiver, 1994*)

"Man-of-war off our stern, Captain, and coming full sail!" (*Beloved Avenger, 1989*)

Wulf Thorsson stood beneath a thickening gray sky in the stern of the Sea Serpent. (*Unwilling Betrayer*, 1992)

Hope yearned to close her eyes, but she dared not. (*Beloved Intruder*, 1992)

Adam was filled with the sheer aching sweetness of having his wife in his arms once more. (*Beloved Pretender*, 1993)

"Hold it right there, lady." Erin Kelly turned and caught her breath at the sight of the man striding so rapidly toward her. (writing as Marianna Essex, *Torrent of Love*, 1983)

"Gretchen! It IS you!" The voice was deep, very distinctive and the shock of hearing it again, so unexpectedly and after such a long time, caused a shower of sparks to flood Gretchen Amsdell's body. (writing as Marianna Essex, *Love Came Courting*, 1984)

In my current work in progress, I knew what the hook was before I'd even plotted the story! Go figure. The opener is:

Something was wrong.

Sir Arthur C. Clarke

Your simple request has opened a large can of worms, which are now squirming on my desk...

I suppose the most famous opening sentence in Anglo-English literature is **"Call me Ishmael."** But why should this be? I'd always believed it was because Ishmael was some kind of wanderer or outcast—but I've just looked him up in the encyclopaedia and find he was a respected Rabbi! So why did Melville choose this name? I've been dredging my memory for opening lines that I remember in some seventy years of omnivorous reading and I can only recall one—from a book I have not opened for half a century, but which made a tremendous impact on me—and perhaps changed my life:

We have explored to its remotest wildernesses a region that all but a few hold to be inaccessible to the human mind. (*The Time Stream*—John Taine) (E.T. Bell)

Meanwhile, here are my two favorites from my own scribbling:

It is three thousand light-years to the Vatican. (*The Star*)

Behind every man now alive stand thirty ghosts. (*2001: A Space Odyssey*)

Margaret (Meg) Chittenden
http://users.techline.com/megc

Openings are very important. Readers tend to expect Lights, Camera, Action nowadays. I'm not fond of the term "narrative hook" all the same, although it is tossed around a lot at writers' conferences. It always sounds phony to me. When I was reading manuscripts for beginning writers, I'd often see a "narrative hook" that had nothing whatever to do with the subsequent story, but was merely tossed in for dramatic effect.

I want something to be happening at the start of my novel. Something exciting if possible, but it doesn't have to be a shoot-out or a fist-fight. Mostly I want my beginnings to be interesting.

Usually, the beginning will occur to me when I'm planning the novel. I write a very complete synopsis before starting the actual writing. Somewhere along the way the beginning just comes to me. Not a very scientific description of the process, but a truthful one.

I try to start with more than one person on scene, in what the old Romans called "In Medias Res" -- in the midst of things. As in *Dead Beat and Deadly*, the third novel in my Charlie Plato Mystery Series.

"Back off," I yelled.

"Louder," the instructor said.

> **I filled my lungs with air, exploded it out through my mouth. "BACK OFF!"**

Some writers would have implied that this was a real life threat that was going on, rather than the self-defense course it happened to be. But that would be cheating the reader and I don't believe in doing that.

So I try to be interesting, and fair, and to use words that will draw the reader into the scene that opens the story.

Here's a different kind of opening from *Dying to Sing*, the first book in the series.

> **It was August 23rd. It had been the kind of unusually warm hazy day Bay area old-timers call earthquake weather.**
>
> **A shrewd bunch, those old-timers.**

I'm also fond of rather mystifying openings.

> **It wasn't a bad feeling, rather like drifting. She was shrinking away from the borders that defined her body, dwindling into a shining molecule. She could see her Andrea-shape looming around her--convex here, concave there—a dim, elongated shadow with appendages she finally recognized as arms and legs.** (*Forever Love*)

These openings are not terribly exciting, but each creates a question in the reader's mind. "Is there going to be an earthquake?" "Why is this woman learning to yell, "Back Off!" "What's going on here?" The reader would read on, I think. And that's the whole idea.

Walter Satterthwait
http://freenet.vcu.edu/education/literature/Walter_Satterthwait.html

I'm flattered that you thought of asking me for input for your next book. But I'm afraid that I'm probably the wrong person to ask. Recently I've been finding those intentionally "hooking" sentences a pain in the neck. There are a number of writers who really go out of their way to set up some elaborate, deliberately jarring opening:

> **Foxwell had nearly finished field stripping his Uzi when he got hit by the plummeting dwarf.**

I find it mannered, and annoying. Zippy opening sentences are often a swell thing, but the idea has lately taken root that they're absolutely necessary; and I think that this notion comes from television, where the opening to a series episode has to be a real grabber, or the poor boob watching it will hit the remote before the commercial demands his limited attention. And recently, when I read one of those things, I tend to toss the book.

It seems to me that a book doesn't have to open with a bang. It can even open with a whimper, so long as the whimper is moderately interesting. The zippy grabber of an opener always suggests to me a book in which the author is a) manipulating me, and in an obvious way; and b) setting up one of those sprightly, bouncy sort of books in which the plot leaps merrily about from place to place as its theoretically lovable eccentric characters are put through their zany paces. Those sort of books are, for me, initially tiresome, quickly annoying, and soon disposed of.

Jonnie Jacobs
http://www.NMOMysteries.com or http://www.zott.com/nmo/main.htm

> **Mixing business and friendship is always something of an iffy proposition, even when you expect things to go smoothly. I had no such expectation where Mona Sterling was concerned.** (*Murder Among Friends*, a Kate Austen mystery)

> **It started with my father's death and nearly ended with my own, though both these events were somewhat peripheral to the murders that rocked the town of Silver Creek early last summer.** (*Shadow of Doubt*, a Kali O'Brien mystery)

In eight years of practicing law, I'd never had a client who gave me the creeps. (*Evidence of Guilt*, a Kali O'Brien)

There's no single right way to hook the reader. Most of us, when we are first introduced to the idea of hooks, assume we need an explosion or a dead body in the first paragraph. While an action-packed opening will get most readers' attention, it's not necessary, or even appropriate for many books.

With my openings, I strive for three things. First, I want to give the reader a sense of the book's tone. There's nothing to be gained by hooking the reader with a highly suspenseful explosion if the rest of the book is going to be romantic comedy. Second, I want the reader to identify in some way with the character or sentiment. Speaking for myself as a reader, I'd find little to draw me to an opening about CIA espionage during the cold war. Third, and most important, I want to raise questions in the reader's mind - questions that will keep him or her reading further.

The opening sentences above are consistent with the casual, almost conversational tone of the books and they touch on a personal sentiment that will (hopefully) give the readers something to identify with. They also raise questions - Who is Mona Sterling and why does the narrator expect trouble? What murders rocked the town of Silver Creek? Who is this new client who gives our narrator the creeps, and why?

An effective opening doesn't have to hit the reader between the eyes, only tickle his mind.

E. C. Ayres
http://members.aol.com/ecayres/home.htm

Having learned my craft in the film and television industries (and in college writing short stories) I would be foolish to disregard the modern convention of the "hook." However, I do at times yearn for the days of subtle hors d'ouvres, followed by more and spicier fare as the reader becomes accustomed to the time, place, and characters. One of the rules I learned in the film business was that there should be no meaningful dialogue at all at the beginning of a film (exposition dialogue, it was called) because the audience was simply too busy getting acclimated to absorb it. Also, I have trouble with the idea, especially with mystery writers, that some obscenely violent and bloody incident is necessary at the outset, to captivate a reader's interest.

All that being said, here are three openings of mine. The first is from my third book, *Night of the Panther*:

> **It's a funny thing, loneliness. It eats away at your spirits like unseen cancer of the soul, until there is nothing left but tattered, fading hopes. And then those, too, are gone. That's how Marge sometimes felt, when darkness closed in on the swamp on nights like this....**

And this from my first book, *Hour of the Manatee*:

> **The blue heron's cry pierced the morning air along the bay front, sending a flock of great white egrets scurrying to wing from the shoreline, where they had been scouting the tidal flats for crabs.**
>
> **Another sound echoed across the waters as the air suddenly began to vibrate with a swelling, thumping, grinding rhythm. It grew, alien to the landscape, more intense. More birds took flight. Even the ever-restless mullet seemed to hesitate and seek cover, leaving the surface waters still as glass...**

Neither is what you would call an action opener, tending towards establishing setting and atmosphere first, but with a sense of something coming.

Off the Shelf

Cassie Raintree was dying of brain cancer every afternoon at 2:30.
James W. Hall, *Bones of Coral*, 1991

"Some of these people *want* to get killed," said Dickie Cruyer as he jabbed the brake pedal to avoid hitting a newsboy.
Len Deighton, *Mexico Set*, 1985

The devil clutched a bomb in his left hand, a pitchfork in his right, and smirked impishly.
Clive Cussler, *Dragon*, 1990

She just might murder her.
Iris Johansen, *And Then You Die...*, 1998

"I knew what it was when I heard the shots."
Edna Buchanan, *Suitable for Framing*, 1995

Saturday, the last day of August I started work before dawn.
Patricia Cornwell, *All that Remains*, 1992

"Wait a minute," he said. "How old are you?"
Sheila Bosworth, *Slow Poison*, 1992

After the first hundred years, some people stop taking chances.
Joe Haldeman, *Buying Time*, 1989

The trouble with an Orphanage upbringing is that when the College discharges you at age eighteen you are burstingly healthy, educated to the edge of intellectual indigestion, and as innocent of day to day reality as a blind dummy.
George Turner, *Brain Child*, 1991

It is Nathan's fault that I became God.
Andrew M. Greeley, *God Game*, 1986

On the last day of his life he read a warning in his horoscope and cast the newspaper aside when a woman asked if she might share the beach.
Andrew Coburn, *Voices in the Dark*, 1994

The town of Lake Minnesota, lies on the shore against Adam's Hill, looking east across the blue-green water to the dark woods.
Garrison Keillor, *Lake Wobegon Days*, 1985

The tiny house must have been white at one time, before fierce Kansas summers checked and blistered the paint, and Kansas winters scoured it down to the raw timber.
Dwight Bennett, *The Guns of Ellsworth*, 1973

"Rocky, would you take a look at this?"
John Varley, *Titan*, 1979

Theodore is in the ground.
Caleb Carr, *The Alienist*, 1994

"Are you sure this is the right road?"
Anthony Bruno, *Bad Business*, 1991

Leaving Missouri had been a last hope--an admission of defeat--with death stalking the way.
Jay Shane, *They Called Him a Fox with Six-Guns*, 1971

Even to a high-flying bird this was a country to be passed over quickly.
Max Brand, The Untamed, 1978

Nobody thinks about death on a nice spring day.
Ed McBain, *Ten Plus One*, 1963

If the Statue of Liberty and Uncle Sam had come together for a one-night stand, guess who would have popped out nine months later? Charlie Blair, Special Agent, FBI. What an American!
Susan Isaacs, *Red, White and Blue*, 1998

Marilyn Meredith
http://fictionforyou.com

I'm a great believer in beginning your novel when something is happening. If you do that, your opening sentences will entice your reader to continue on with the story.

In the first of my Deputy Tempe Crabtree mystery series, *Deadly Omen*, I began like this:

> **"I know what I heard! A dog howled all night long. We both know what that means."**

Of course, the reader probably doesn't know, and hopefully will want to find out by reading more.

The second in the series, *Unequally Yoked*, begins this way:

"My little girl's gone! You gotta find her." With arms flailing, the woman ran toward Tempe as she climbed out of her official white Blazer.

Again, there's a compelling reason to continue on.

As an instructor for the novel section of Writer's Digest School, I urge my students to create opening sentences that will instantly hook their readers.

C. J. Cherryh
http://www.cherryh.com

Opening lines have never been that definite for me: I just deal with them as I do any other line in the book, so I can't think of any that are particularly showy without thinking of a whole book.

Michael H. Payne
http://www.kuci.org/~mpayne/

To tell the truth, I don't seem to use hook-type openings. I like mild, unassuming opening lines that set a gentle, normal scene. Then I use the next few lines to twist that normalcy. For instance, here's how my story "A Bag of Custard" opens:

> **It was late Friday afternoon when my dog Bruce walked Into the front room carrying a paper sack in his jaws. He put it on the floor, looked up at me with his big, brown eyes, and said, "Look, Jim, I've got to go out of town for the weekend. Could you watch my bag for me?"**
>
> **I had just come in, hadn't even undone my tie yet, and all I could do for a minute was sit on the couch and stare at him; I mean, this wasn't normal behavior for a Lab-Doberman mix.**

Or the opening from my story "One Thin Dime:"

> **It was the thump-thump-thump of those paws on her chest that woke Donna more than the frenzied**

shouting: "Donna! I've been robbed! I've been robbed!"

"What?!" Donna sat up with a start and felt the weight fall from her chest into her lap. "What?!"

A breeze sprang up in front of her, two dots of red whirling into view. "Thieves!" the voice rang out in the darkness. "Thieves! Right here! In this apartment!"

Donna slapped at the lamp on her nightstand and squinted into the light that flooded the room. Above her blankets rustled the little dragon, his eyes spinning, his wings a green blur. As her mind began to focus, she managed to ask, "What are you talking about, Lance?"

The dragon zoomed into her face and held out a paw, claws extended. "Five dimes from my hoard, Donna! Gone! Do you hear me?! Stolen!" His eyes blazed. "You've been dipping in for bus fare again, haven't you? Haven't you?!"

Off the Shelf

Later, I found out his name was John Daggett, but that's not how he introduced himself the day he walked into my office.
Sue Grafton, *'D' is for Deadbeat,* 1987

The case began quietly, on the women's floor of the county jail.
Ross Macdonald, *The Ferguson Affair,* 1960

Ryll felt no pain on awakening and he did not remember the collision.
Frank Herbert and Brian Herbert, *Man of Two Worlds,* 1986

It was an old plane, a four-engine plasma jet that had been retired from active service and it came in along about that it was neither economical nor particularly safe.
Isaac Asimov, *Fantastic Voyage,* 1966

Saturday A.M. It was a thin scream; the empty street and the night silence briefly nurtured it, then it was sucked up between the high-rise buildings like smoke up a flue and wafted away across a starless sky.
Lillian O'Donnell, *After-Shock*, 1977

Anna knew that he was doing his best to be interested.
Maeve Binchy, *Silver Wedding*, 1989

Stephen was watching the two girls, though they were not aware of it.
Malcolm MacDonald, *A Woman Alone*, 1990

Ron Goulart

I've been fascinated with hooks ever since I discovered them sometime during my teenage years. I think Frederic Brown, especially in his science fiction stories, was one of the first writers I noticed using them. In college I had an English professor who maintained that the meaning, structure and direction of a book could be, if you were skillful enough, contained in the opening paragraph. He was talking about nonfiction, but it occurred to me at the time that that could also apply to fiction.

When I worked in the advertising business in my youth, we also wanted to hook the reader or the listener with the first couple of lines of copy. I had a copychief who'd hold his thumb and forefinger about an inch apart—"That's how much space you have to grab them." Though I'm not as crass as I was during my ad days, I still adhere to some of the rules I learned back several decades ago.

Over the years I became increasingly fascinated with trying to devise a hook that was exactly one line long. Some of them are just teasers and some actually attempt to hint at the entire story in that opening line.

Here are a couple of examples of this latter approach.

It wasn't really an earthquake that caused the ground to open and swallow the second most popular child star in Hollywood. (*The Curse of the Demon*)

As it turned out, he didn't get a chance to murder anybody. (*Believing in Santa*)

With hooks like these, what I have to do is go around in a circle and by the end of the story reach the point where I started. Only this time the reader, I fervently hope, now understands what the opening line meant.

Here are some examples of the just plain teaser hook.

He took another walk around the dead man. (*Keep It Clean*)

It was about a half hour after the second bomb scare that his real trouble got going. (*A Cure for Baldness*)
Movies and folklore to the contrary, sudden and profound changes in your size can be both advantageous and a great deal of fun. (*Downsized*)

It was about the time that the third large fire-spitting demon came spilling out of the bathtub that I decided to capitulate. (*Why I Never Went Steady With Heather Moon*)

This last one illustrates another way to use a hook. You open in the middle of the story and show your focal character already tangled up with his problem. Then, as the narrative starts to move forward, you also fill in the details as to how he got so fouled up—in this case with demons.

Of course, there is a danger for a writer in becoming too hooked on hooks. The story itself won't be able to live up to the opening lines. Still, I find them worth the risk and wouldn't abandon the habit now even if I could.

Here's one final hook I throw in because it's the opening of the first novel in my latest mystery series:

The world wasn't in especially good shape that autumn of 1937. And I ought to know, I was there. (*Groucho Marx, Master Detective*)

Dennis L. McKiernan
http://home.att.net/~dlmck

I think I'm not different from other writers, in that I'd like my opening lines to cause the reader to want to turn the page and go on. I've always tried to hew to the principal that the most important chapter in a book is the first one; and the most important paragraph is the first one in chapter one; and the most important sentence is the first one in the first paragraph in the opening chapter. Of course, to back up that opening, I need a good story to tell, and to tell it well. Hence, there are many other things that the writer needs to concentrate on other than just opening lines, for not only does the writer need to grab the reader, s/he needs to hold the reader, too. From the opening line to the closing one, and not only should the reader be dragged into the story, but s/he needs to be held in thrall by what comes after. That said ... Some of my opening lines have been:

> **Lightning stroked the night, the glare flaring through the narrow windows, thunder rolling after. As if summoned by the flash, a blast of rain hammered down on the small, ramshackle, dockside tavern, while the wind rattled door and sideboards and slammed a loose shutter to and fro, and waves roared against the pilings 'neath.**

> **Inside the weatherworn building the sound of the storm was muted somewhat, and Olar, his elbows on the rough broad plank which served as a bar, leaned forward and hissed to Trig, "Wha' be them two women doin' here, eh?" He thrust his narrow chin sideways toward the shadow-wrapped corner where the two strangers sat just beyond the yellow light of the single tavern lantern hanging above the bar. "Mayhap a couple o' doxies come t' ply their trade when th' raiders return, aye?"**

> **Tryg, proprietor of the Cove, snorted at Olar's remark, then leaned forward and said in a voice just loud enough to be heard above the moan of the wind and drum of the rain and the rattle and bang and swash,**

"Ye'd better not let them hear ye call 'em doxies, laddie, else ye're like to come up missing y'r balls."

Yngli, the only other person in the tavern, slapped the plank and laughed at this remark, but Olar looked at Tryg in surprise. "'N' j'st why d'ye say that?"

"'Cause one o' them be an Elf, 'n' t'other's a, a, well I don't rightly know her kind, yet she be th' one wi' th' gleamin' swords."

Olar drew his breath in through clenched teeth and glanced toward the shadows of the darkened corner as lightning again stroked nearby, thunder slapping after. The flare briefly illuminated the outsiders' faces: delicate, strange, exotic. The one on the left was fair skinned--ivory and alabaster--and she had hazel eyes aslant and chestnut locks falling to her shoulders, with pointed-tipped ears showing through. The one on the right was saffron skinned--tawny, ivory yellow--her tilted eyes glittered onyx, her short-cropped raven-black hair shone glossy . . . but this one's ears were not tipped.

The strangers sat in the corner with their backs to the wall, silent, impassive, as if waiting. On the table before the yellow one lay two unsheathed swords, one long, one shorter, each slightly curved; the blades glinted wickedly as lightning flared. (*The Dragonstone*)

In the foregoing, I use the storm to evoke an image of elemental violence, and through Olar I ask a question concerning two women who seem out of place, yet women who bear weapons, exotic women at that. As to Olar's question, it is one that I hope will get the reader to wondering just what those two females are doing in this ramshackle place, and I hope the reader will want to follow the story long enough to find the answer, and by the time that happens, I believe the reader will not only be hooked, but will be landed as well.

As you can see, I try to evoke moods and to catch the reader's curiosity in my story openings, and if I can do so ... well, you know what follows. But remember, not only must the reader turn the next page and the next, s/he must keep on turning the pages all the way through to the end. Hence, the author must have a good story to tell and to tell it well.

Denise Turney
http://www.chistell.com

I know this piece is about opening lines, but I for one decide whether to read or not to read a story based on the opening paragraphs. One line simply does not tell me enough about the story to make a decision to or not to buy the book or to keep reading the book after I have bought it or checked it out of the library.

A good opener should give the reader a gist of what the book is about. An opener should not be a tease. Meaning - an opener should not be written to entice and grab the reader's interest IF the rest of the story is flat. To give examples of the effect openers have on readers I have typed two different openings for my next book - "When What Shouldn't Be Is". The book will start with the second opener. The second opener provides more information and intrigue. It sets the tone for the book.

> First Opener: **Robin tightened her grip on the shopping bag handle. She grit her teeth and thought about Leslie. She hoped she wasn't home.**

> **"Wanted. Roommate. Single female artist, between the ages of 20-35 to share living expenses with local actress. Must be a woman with a job, no kids, and her own car. Race unimportant." The words kept playing in her head. They were the words she believed Leslie used to trap an unsuspecting New Yorker - her.**

> Second Opener: **"Wanted. Roommate. Single female artist, between the ages of 20-35 to share living expenses with local actress. Must be a woman with a steady job, no kids, and her own car. Race unimportant." Robin tightened her grip on the shopping bag handle. She grit her teeth and thought**

about Leslie. She hoped she wasn't home. The words to the ad she answered one year ago kept playing in her head. They were the words she believed Leslie used to trap an unsuspecting New Yorker - her. Confusion poisoned her life now. Loud, drug addicted men. Alcoholic rages. Angry bill collectors ringing the bell and calling on the telephone. And now death threats. So much changed in her life since she moved in with Leslie. (*When What Should Be Is*)

Masters of the craft tend to be avid readers. The more you read, the more readily you can separate a good story from a flat story. If an opening doesn't interest you as the writer of the story, it most likely will not interest anyone else. I know once I get beyond the critic that is called "me," for the most part I am home free.

Frederik Pohl

I think the opening lines of mine that I like best are from my novel, *Gateway*, which, as it happens, is also the novel of mine that I'm most contented with in general:

My name is Robinette Broadhead, in spite of which I am male. My analyst (whom I call Sigfrid von Shrink, although that isn't his name; he hasn't got a name, being a machine) has a lot of electronic fun with this fact:

"Why do you care if some people think it's a girl's name, Bob?"

"I don't."

"Then why do you keep bringing it up?"

The best part of this opening is that it moves the reader directly into the story to come. In more than thirty years as an editor I was exposed to a good many thousands, or perhaps tens of thousands, of opening lines. The cutesy ones (i.e., "After the T. rex caught me I could feel it crushing my skull in its teeth. So I was surprised, the next morning, to find myself eating scones and Devonshire cream with the Secretary-General of the U.N.") usually did their job in getting me to read the next few pages, all right. But unless there was an actual story building by then I generally stopped reading and sent the manuscript back.

Are opening lines important? Somewhat so, yes; at least it is definitely better to have an intriguing opening than one that actively turns the readers off. But unless the story carries its weight no opening line will save it.

Off the Shelf

Well, preacher, if you've come to pray over me in my last hours, I'm afraid it's too late.
Lee McElroy, *Joe Pepper*, 1975

There are various ways of mending a broken heart, but perhaps going to a learned conference is one of the more unusual.
Barbara Pym, *No Fond Return of Love*, 1961

One thing about Montana, you could watch rain coming a long way off.
Carter Travis Young, *The Pocket Hunters*, 1972

The map under glass made no sense.
Nicholas Jose, *Avenue of Eternal Peace*, 1991

Heaven knows, I never meant any of this to happen.
Richard Powell, *Don Quixote, U.S.A.*, 1966

I had even reached the point of wondering if Geraldine Vrevoort's suicide, so long dreaded, might not prove in the event a relief, but like everything else about Geraldine, when it came, it came with a nasty twist.
Louis Auchincloss, *Portrait in Brownstone*, 1962

He wasn't a small man, but he walked small.
Paula Gosling, *Solo Blues*, 1981

The first time I saw the publisher's daughter she wore slippers and a couple of scant strips of black cloth and a cigarette.
Bruno Fischer, *The Lady Kills*, 1951

If her mind had not been on the case she had won, Katie might not have taken the curve so fast, but the intense satisfaction of the guilty verdict was still absorbing her.
Mary Higgins Clark, *The Cradle Will Fall*, 1980

Grayson Albemarle St. Cyre, Baron Cliffe, read the single page one more time, then slowly crumpled it in his hand.
Catherine Coulter, *Mad Jack*, 1999

There are no hundred percent heroes.
John D. MacDonald, *Cinnamon Skin*, 1982

He looked down, confusedly wondering where he was as a person does when he awakens in a strange place.
Don Coldsmith, *The Flower in the Mountain*, 1988

"I'm pregnant."
Sandra Brown, *Tidings of Great Joy*, 1987

At six minutes past midnight, Tuesday morning, on the way home from a late rehearsal of her stage show, Tina Rvans saw her son, Danny, in a stranger's car.
Dean Koontz, *The Eyes of Darkness*, 1981

It was two days before the opening of school when the Spanish teacher dropped dead.
Beth Gutcheon, *Saying Grace*, 1995

First, I closed the windows and bolted the flimsy aluminum door.
Charles Willeford, *Cockfighter*, 1972

It wasn't easy establishing myself as Palm Beach's leading practitioner of "gross moral misconduct," to borrow a phrase from the court's final judgment in my divorce.
Rozanne Pulitzer with Kathleen Maxa, *The Prize Pulitzer*, 1987

From the verandah where she had been left to wait she could see the golf course adjoining the hospital grounds.
Kenneth Millar, *The Three Roads*, 1958

Her knuckles stood out white against the tan of her clenched hands.
Susan Dunlap, *Rogue Wave*, 1991

"Who is John Galt?"
Ayn Rand, *Atlas Shrugged*, 1957

A peculiar ritual took place every evening when Wilma Rathjen came home from work.
Helen Nielsen, *The Woman on the Roof*, 1954

"It was in my hair, Severian," Dorcas said.
Gene Wolfe, *The Sword of the Lictor*, 1981

The naked child ran out of the hide-covered lean-to toward the rocky beach at the bend in the small river.
Jean M. Auel, *The Clan of the Cave Bear*, 1980

I met the boy on the morning of the kidnapping.
Ross Macdonald, *Meet Me at the Morgue*, 1953

The last thing Raymond Gaver expected was that he would die with a key to the Beverly Hills Hotel in his pocket.
Beth Gutcheon, *Domestic Pleasures*, 1991

The gem colored dream shattered and left the kid gaping on the street.
Joan D. Vinge, *Alien Blood*, 1982

A.D. 1892 Cloud covered the sky like a gray stone plate.
Larry Niven, *The Ringworld*, 1996

Mainstream Authors' Pseudonyms

Pseudonym	Author Name
Mark Twain	Samuel Clemens
Lewis Carroll	Charles Lutwidge Dodgson
David Durham	Roy Vickers
S.S. VanDine	Williard Huntington Wright
Voltaire	Francois Marie Aroult
O. Henry	William Sydney Porter

5 -- Set the Mood

A story's opening provides the framework for the entire theme. The components may include an engrossing plot, and likely a subplot as well; believable characters, especially a hero or heroine the reader can identify with; credible and consistent details for the time chosen (such as a Gothic romance, the future on a different planet, and so on); conflict, action, reaction, and interaction in the form of realistic dialogue and gestures.

Once the mood is set, the author must follow through. Setting the mood is even more difficult than it sounds. Of course, the pros make it look simple. Read on to see how they set their scenes and moods.

Insights

Harlen Campbell
http://www.highfiber.com/~campbell/

How to begin? Jump right into the story? An explosion, death, an orphan pursued. . . ? Imply an unexpiated guilt sweeping across a generation, from a public war to an equally violent, if more private, aftermath?

No. Wrong tone. This is a novel. I've 400 pages to fill. Time to dwell on character a bit, because character is central. Fate, the Greeks believed, is character, and it certainly is in the story I want to tell, so... look at the character, then. Give him his particular place in the world and let that place, freely chosen, elaborate his character. But be careful not to place him in a vacuum. He needs a setting that mirrors what war, time, and guilt have made of him. What he's made of himself. What he wishes he'd made of himself.

Start with setting and character. This is a man who allows himself no peace, who pushes, always pushes. A runner, perhaps, but not a man who runs in company. One who runs alone, who keeps a wary eye to his back and a comfortable distance between himself and the crowd. The setting should show that in him, but it mustn't make him a hermit, for the only meaningful action is human action and the only story worth telling is a human story, so. . . .
How to begin?

> **The road to my house twists up the west face of the northern end of the Sandia Mountains, doubling back on itself in a number of hairpin curves. It is a hard run. I run it every day, and as I jog, the occasional breaks in the pine and cedar forest on either side offer a comfortable hundred-mile perspective on the human race.**

K.D. Wentworth
http://www.ionet.net/~richard-11/

From "Burning Bright," *Aboriginal SF*, Summer, 1996, Nebula Finalist Story, 1997:

> **I surprised Phil Ferguson at the bend of the sluggish green river. He looked up, his cheeks shimmering with iridescent fire; at some point in the last week, he had obviously stopped taking his preventative. I didn't know what to say. The Survey manual was crammed with protocol on how to avoid contamination from native life-forms, but it didn't say a damn thing about idiots who sought it like a form of salvation.**

I like to start a story at the point of differentiation from our own reality, whenever possible, in order to grab the reader's attention.

This opening delineates the story problem in just a few sentences and provides clues about time, place, and the characters, always critical in an SF or fantasy story. How are this setting and time different from our own? How do these people think? What is the mood and how will I color the voice of the narrative? These are all questions to consider in writing opening lines.

William Sanders
http://www.sff.net/people/sanders/index.htp

> **"It was a dark and stormy night - and I know, God damn it, but I can't help it, it was."** William Sanders, *A Death on 66*

I always considered that my best opening line. A lot of people seemed to agree.

However, SF and fantasy fans would probably hold out for my openers (two sentences, technically, so sue me) in *Journey to Fusang*:

> **And how was I to know she was the High King's own daughter? Besides, she swore she was fifteen.**

Then too you might like the opening lines of my newest, *The Ballad of Billy Badass and the Rose of Turkestan,* (1999):

> **Billy Badass was sitting on a big rock above Barren Fork Creek when his grandfather spoke to him for the first time. Or rather it was the first time in the five years since his grandfather had died.**

Robert Weinberg
http://www.sff.net/people/r.weinberg

A good opening line is like a firm handshake. It needs to be self-assured while being not too strong nor too weak. Most of all, it needs to make a vivid impression. I work very hard on my first lines. I read them over and over again until they are exactly right. To me, writing is storytelling, and I feel that anything I put down on paper should sound as good as it reads. I always keep that thought in mind as I compose my work, and I've never submitted a story without reading it aloud first. If it doesn't sound right, then it's not ready. And, that first line, the line used to capture the reader's attention, to make him want to read more, must resonate like the ringing of a bell.

My personal favorite first line of all my stories and novels comes from a short story titled "The Midnight El," published in *Return to the Twilight Zone*.

> **Cold and alone, Sidney Taine waited for the Midnight El.**

Not long, not complex, but it reads right. There's drama in that line, and it raises a number of questions that hopefully will push the reader to continue. Who is Taine and why is he cold and alone? More important, what is the Midnight El? Most of all, it sets the mood - somber, chilling, dark. It works. Which is all any writer can ask from a first line.

Larry Niven

My correspondence course in writing told me about narrative hooks. The purpose of a hook is to keep the reader reading, but in my stranger stories the hook must also ease him into an imaginary world without confusion. Do it right and his sense of wonder will pull him right in: he can see most of what's going on, and he'll kill to learn the rest.

Oath of Fealty, written with Jerry Pournelle, was published in 1981. Here is what a building two miles long by two wide by a fifth of a mile high looks like to three college kids about to break in.

> **Elsewhere in Los Angeles it was late afternoon, but here was only twilight. The three invaders peering out of the orange grove were deep in shadow. The sky blazed behind them and sent chinks of blue-white light through the trees to make the shadows darker. There was a fresh smell of fertilizers and crushed orange peel carried on the warm Santa Ana wind.**

Close ahead the eastern face of Todos Santos was a black wall across the world. Thousands of balconies and windows in neat array showed in this light as no more than a faceless void seen through gray leaves, a sharp-edged black rectangle blotting out the sun.

…"Bad for the guards, too," said the girl. "It's late afternoon everywhere but here. At night they'd *know* they couldn't see…."

Todos Santos is only an arcology, but it's big enough to create its own climate…and that shapes the invasion.

My readers are very familiar with the *Ringworld* and with the Kzinti and Pierson's puppeteer species. *The Ringworld Throne* must show it all again, explain it all to the new readers without losing the old. Sequels are always like that.

But I thought of something new for the puppeteer character, the Hindmost:

The Hindmost danced.

They were dancing as far as the eye could see, beneath a ceiling that was a flat mirror. Tens of thousands of his kind moved in tight patterns that were great mutating curves, heads cocked high and low to keep their orientation. The clicking of their hooves was a part of the music, like a hundred thousand castanets.

Kick short, kick past, veer. One eye for your counterpartner. In this movement and the next, never glance toward the wall that hides the Brides.

Never touch.

Odd shape and strange gender patterns just showing through. Now the Hindmost calls Louis Wu (the man) and Chmeee (the Kzin) and resumes their dominance game. He broke communication during The Ringworld Engineers. Now he uses the dance to distract them: they are not to see the oddness of his call.

Rainbow Mars picks up a character I haven't touched in 25 years. A new reader will need the background; a familiar reader doesn't want to be bored. So:

> **+390 Atomic Era. Svetz was nearly home, but the snake was waking up.**
>
> **Gravity pulled outward from the center of the extension cage as it was pulled toward present time. The view through the wall was a jitter of color and motion. Svetz lay on his back and looked up at the snake. A filter helmet showed only as a faint golden glow around its head. It wouldn't strangle on post-Industrial air, and it couldn't bite him through the inflated bubble.**
>
> **A ripple ran down the feathers along its spine, a gaudy flurry of color, nine meters from head to tip of tail. It seemed to take forever. Tiny rainbow-colored wings fluttered at its neck. Its eyes opened.**
>
> **The natives of -550 Atomic Era would have carved his heart out without losing that same look of dispassionate arrogance.**
>
> **Here it all is: the Institute for Temporal Research, time travel, polluted air and species lost to 3100 AD, strange creatures brought back for the Secretary-General's Zoo, and Svetz, still unaware that time travel is fantasy.**

For the Prologue for *The Burning City*, by me and Jerry Pournelle, due in 1999 from Simon & Schuster/Pocket, I did Omniscient Author. This is dangerous, but it's easier in fantasy.

> **There was fire on Earth before the fire god came. There has always been fire. What Prokeet gave to mankind was madness.**
>
> **Prokeet's children will play with fire even after they burn their fingers.**
>
> **It was only Prokeet's joke, then and for unmeasured time after. But a greater god called**

down the great cold, and Prokeet's joke came into
its own. In the icy north men could not survive
unless the fire god favored one of their number.

Cautious men and women never burned
themselves twice; but their people died of the
cold. Someone must tend the fire during the
terrible winters. Twelve thousand years before the
birth of Christ, when most of the gods had gone
mythical and magic was fading from the world,
Prokeet's gift remained. Some people like to play
with fire.

My themes throughout the book will be myths, the deep past, fire
and the fire god, pyromania and its origins...and the south-central
Los Angeles Riots played out fourteen thousand years early.

I think I'm getting better at this.

Jaclyn Reding
http://www.inficad.com/~jacreding/

For me opening lines and scenes are very important. I
seek either to immediately grab the reader's attention with a jolt, or
in other cases (depending on each story), set more of the mood
before drawing the reader curiously into the story.

Lord Noah Edenhall didn't stir an inch from his relaxed
position in the comfortable caffoy-covered wing chair
set before the blazing hearth. His booted feet stayed
stretched at full-length before him. His chin remained
as it was, resting placidly upon his fist. The cuff of his
navy cutaway still barely brushed his knuckles as he
regarded his friend, his closest friend in life, over their
respective brandy glasses. A moment passed, then
two. Still he simply stared. And then finally,
incredulously, he said past the scowl crossing his
mouth, "Surely you have gone even madder than the
old king this time, Tony." (*White Magic*)

For the above first example...I was setting more a mood here of
relaxation before "zinging" it with the hero's accusation that his

friend has gone mad. I wanted to make the reader as comfortable as the character seemed to be before leading into the dialogue that would follow.

With this next one I was hoping to immediately intrigue the reader with the heroine's grand plan, her very motivation for the entire story, while also showing the importance of the occasion to the character herself.

> **It was the thirtieth of July, 1658, the summer of her twenty-third year, and she couldn't have asked for a better day on which to start the Plan.** (*Tempting Fate*)

Well, this one sort of speaks for itself...

> **Breathing, hot and heavy and blowing just beside the lobe of her left ear. It was that sound which first woke Gillian from sleep.** (*Stealing Heaven*)

But my all-time favorite of my opening lines is from my novel in *White Wings (1999)*:

> **The aging duke's eyes brightened as he openly appraised her figure. "Tell me, girl, are your breasts genuine?"**

Robert J. Sawyer
www.sfwriter.com

> **My father is dying.** *(End of an Era, 1994)*

I've always liked really short opening lines -- something the bookstore browser's eye takes in all at once. I think that's a much more effective grab than a paragraph-long sentence that requires the browser to consciously read in order to absorb.

I'm fond of this particular opening for several reasons. First, *End of an Era* is a time-travel novel about dinosaurs; I knew that the cover would show a prehistoric landscape. And yet, no matter how far out the premises in my SF novels get, I always strive for a human quality and I wanted to drive home immediately that there was more to this book than just action-adventure, so I felt the juxtaposition of the cover art and that sentence would be quite effective.

I don't often write in the first person, but if you are going to do so, I figure you should take full advantage of the immediacy that voice offers right from the opening sentence (a first-person tale could start with description rather than a personal declaration, after all, but I don't think that's nearly as effective).

Finally, as you may have noticed, the sentence is in the present tense, very unusual for fiction; indeed, the whole opening scene in *End of an Era* is present tense. Because the novel plays with past and future, I wanted to start out by immediately jarring the reader's time sense, and I think the tense choice accomplishes that. My own real father -- hale and healthy at seventy when the book was published -- has said that of my dozen novels, *End of an Era* is the only one he hasn't read: the four words of that first sentence were too much for him to bear as written by his own son. I never wanted to upset my father, but I did want the words to have a powerful emotional impact, and many readers have told me that they do.

Off the Shelf

The day started to go a little crazy when Keith Duffy and his young daughter brought that poor crushed doe to the Inn-Patient, as I call my small animal hospital in Bear Bluff, Colorado, about fifty minutes northwest of Boulder along the "Peak-to-Peak" Highway.
James Patterson, *When the Wind Blows*, 1998

Most of the people who come to see Nero Wolfe by appointment, especially from as far away as Nebraska, show some sign of being in trouble, but that one didn't.
Rex Stout, *Might as Well Be Dead*, 1956

Frank Shade had traveled a long way to get nowhere.
Clifton Adams, *The Grabhorn Bounty*, 1965

Something unpleasant was going to happen, something incredibly and overwhelmingly unpleasant.
Craig Rice, *Knocked for a Loop*, 1957

The voice on the telephone seemed to be sharp and peremptory, but I didn't hear too well what it said--partly because I was only half awake and partly because I was holding the receiver upside down.
Raymond Chandler, *Playback*, 1958

Shorty Gibbs lay on the gray edge of consciousness, his eyes tightly closed, trying to guess where he was.
Clifton Adams, *Shorty*, 1966

"Well, frankly it was an accident," Edie Barlow's sister said to her as they sat together over the remains of veal scaloppini.
David Delman, *A Time to Marry*, 1961

Berenice was sixteen years old when she witnessed her father's murder, and she watched the sequence of events that led to it with curious indifference.
Howard Fast, *Agrippa's Daughter*, 1964

On the night he had chosen months before, Malacar Miles crossed the street numbered seven, passing beneath the glow-globe he had damaged during the day.
Roger Zelazny, *To Die in Italbar*, 1973

There was death at its beginning, as there would be death again at its end.
Nicholas Evans, *The Horse Whisperer*

Seven misshapen figures emerged from a blinding swirl of desert sand and sage.
Steven Spielberg, *Close Encounters of the Third Kind*, 1977

Life goes on yes--any fool and his self-respect are soon parted perhaps never to be reunited, even on Judgment Day.
Kurt Vonnegut, *Jailbird*, 1979

"Ah," Jennie McCaine groaned sensuously as she settled her slim, sore body into the hot, steaming bath water.
Bobbi Smith, *Arizona Temptress*, 1986

Of all the rash and midnight promises made in the name of love, none, Boone now knew was more certain to be broken than "I'll never leave you."
Clive Barker, *Cabal*, 1985

Edward D. Hoch

I usually go for a quiet opening, but one that gives a fair amount of information while grabbing the reader's interest. My story "Murder of a Gypsy King" in the July 1998 issue of Ellery Queen's Mystery Magazine begins:

> **On the long, lonely highway into Bucharest that sunny August afternoon, Jennifer Beatty suddenly changed her mind.**

In those few words I tell the readers the time and place of my story as well as the name of a major character in it. More than that, I hope I pique their interest as to what she was doing there, what she changed her mind about, and what happened next as a result of it. Naturally a dark and threatening opening can be even better, but in this regard no one is likely to top Graham Greene's first sentence from *Brighton Rock* (1938):

> **Hale knew, before he had been in Brighton three hours, that they meant to murder him.**

Greg Bear
http://www.gregbear.com

I think the most provocative opening paragraph I've written recently is from my novella "Heads," 1993:

> **Order and cold, heat and politics. The imposition of wrong order: anger, death, suicide, and destruction. I lost loved ones, lost my illusions and went through mental and physical hell, but what still haunts my dreams, thirty years after, are the great silvery refrigerators four stories tall angling motionless in the dark void of the Ice Pit; the force disorder pumps with their constant sucking soundlessness; the dissolving ghost of my sister, Rho; and William Pierce's expression when he faced his lifetime goal, in the Quiet...**

I believe that Rho and William are dead, but I will never be sure. I am even less sure about the four hundred and ten heads.

It's important to me to set the mood and themes, or hint at them, in the first few lines, just to get the reader settled in a chair and ready for the whole experience.

Barbara Paul
http://www.barbarapaul.com/

Sylvia Markey was holding her cat's head in her hands.

Just the head.

Sylvia was swaying on her feet; I didn't feel any too steady myself. A whispered "Jesus Christ" floated from behind me. I snatched Ian Cavanaugh's make-up towel away from him and wrapped up the cat's head, handed the mess to Leo Gunn, the stage manager.

That's the opening of *The Fourth Wall*. I'm satisfied with it because it does three things. First, it establishes the setting (without using the word "theater" -- "make-up towel" and "stage manager" take care of that). Second, it introduces four characters, three of them by name. Third, it presents the initiating incident of the plot (the beheading of the cat).

All that in just four sentences and a fragment. That's the only time I've been able to pack so much into so few words. I'm rather proud of that.

It's also an opening that takes a big risk, because it violates one of those unwritten rules we all know about: you never kill a cat in a mystery. Dogs, horses, people -- okay. But never a cat.

I'm a cat-lover myself; I've got five of the critters. But that's precisely why I chose that incident: it's such a godawful thing to happen. *The Fourth Wall* is a grim story and I needed a grim incident to kick it off. That act of inexcusable cruelty set exactly the right tone.

William C. Dietz

My favorite comes from *Bodyguard*, a science fiction novel published in 1994. The goal was to suggest the setting, set the mood, and say something about the main character (narrator) all in a couple of paragraphs.

We rose from the depths of the Urboplex like a plague of sewer rats, drifting upwards on crowded platforms, riding the humanity packed escalators, or climbing hundreds of stairs to emerge blinking from seldom-used exits.

We were a hard-eyed lot, younger rather than older, and almost universally desperate. For we were the bottom feeders, the lowest ranking members of a long, hard food chain, willing to do what it took to survive, and well aware of the fact that whatever value we had was related to brawn rather than brains. Something I've been short of ever since a portion of mine was blown out during the Battle of Three Moons.

Off the Shelf

Sometimes the hot night wind brings bad dreams.
John D. MacDonald, *Where is Janice Gantry?* 1961

It started with a kid.
Andrew Vachass, *Strega*, 1987

Six days ago, a man blew himself up by the side of a road in northern Wisconsin.
Paul Auster, *Leviathan*, 1992

On a late-winter evening in 1983, while driving through fog along the Maine coast, recollections of old campfires began to drift into the March mist, and I thought of the Abnaki Indians of the Algonquin tribe who dwelt near Bangor a thousand years ago.
Norman Mailer, *Harlot's Ghost*, 1991

By April most people had already forgotten about him, except for some of the nurses on the floor who crossed themselves when they walked past his room.
Alice Hoffman, *Second Nature*, 1994

The girl was pretty enough to make a man fall head over common sense in love, and woman enough to keep him that way.
Patricia Waddell, *Sara's Promise*, 1999

It was a pleasure to burn.
Ray Bradbury, *Fahrenheit 451*, 1951

He'd never particularly liked cats.
Sandra Brown, *Where There's Smoke*, 1993

Ever after, whenever she smelled the peculiar odor of new construction, of pine planking and plastic plumbing pipes, she would think of that summer, think of it as the time of changes.
Anna Quindlen, *Object Lessons*, 1991

Every old house, during a long association with human misfortune, acquires a ghost; the chateau of Chenonceaux is haunted by a queen of France.
David Linzee, *Discretion*, 1977

Hugh Valleroy paced back and forth, heedless of the muddy water he was splashing onto the boots of the District Director of Federal Police.
Jacqueline Lichtenberg, *House of Zeor*, 1974

Exactly three months before the killing at Martingale Mrs. Maxie gave a dinner party.
P.D. James, *Cover Her Face*, 1962

Friday the nineteenth of May was a full day.
Donald Westlake, *God Save the Mark*, 1967

It's perverse!
Robert Bolt, *A Man for All Seasons*, 1960

The idiot lived in a black and gray world, punctuated by the white lightning of hunger and flickering of fear.
Theodore Sturgeon, *More Than Human*, 1952

The call came while I was trying to persuade a lameduck
Congressman to settle his tab before he burned his American
Express card.
Ross Thomas, *Cast a Yellow Shadow*, 1967

In spite of all his efforts, Tavernor was unable to remain indoors
when it was time for the sky to catch fire.
Bob Shaw, *The Palace of Eternity*, 1969

Astronauts hold few charms for psychiatrists.
John Boyd, *The Rakehells of Heaven*, 1969

When the invitation arrived in the mail, I assumed it was a joke.
Jane Heller, *Name Dropping*, 2000

In the hospital of the orphanage--the boys' division at St. Cloud's-
-two nurses were in charge of naming the new babies and
checking that their little penises were healing from the obligatory
circumcision.
John Irving, *Cider House Rules*, 1985

The Turks have dreary jails.
Lawrence Block, *The Thief Who Couldn't Sleep*, 1966

> The most virtuous lady novelists
> write things that would make a bartender blush.
> H.L. Mencken, *Prejudices: Fifth Series*, 1926

The first five of George Bernard Shaw's novels were rejected by
every publisher in London. He switched to writing plays and his
career took off. It was not until many years later, that all
five novels were published and became well sought after. Shaw
admitted they were ramblings rather than good works.
But, the novels proved to be a good way of
teaching Shaw what not to do.

John Moore

http://www.sff.net/people/John.Moore/

In a short story every word counts, so I like to set the scene in the first sentence, and I try to do it so that it sets up the conflict also.

> **The control room was quiet and twilight dark, lit only by blue glow from the monitors, the hash of green LED readouts on the walls, and from the center console, the flashing of a single red emergency light.**

In the second sentence I'll bring in a character and conflict, of course, develops from the character's actions.

> **Neville covered the light with his hand and looked furtively over his shoulder.**

In a novel there's more room to work with, but I'll still set the scene and bring in a major character on the first page.

Deborah Morgan

http://www.lorenestleman.com/deborah_morgan.htm

> **Know your gun.**
>
> **It can make the difference when the smoke clears, or The sun rises, or you're helping someone back through the door that separates humanity from the demons of the dark.**
>
> **Mine's the latest Smith and Wesson Air Lite -- a .22LR snub nose revolver with eight chambers on an aluminum alloy J-frame. It weighs less than a pound, loaded.**
>
> **I didn't know all this shit a week ago. Now, ask me anything. "Freight" (from the anthology, *Lethal Ladies II*)**

Short story writing has its own challenges, the first of which is achieving more than one feat with each sentence. While the novel form is a canvas, the short story form is a picture postcard.

Note that in the opening of "Freight" (which, by the way, debuted my private investigator Mary Shelley), I've foreshadowed things to come by letting the reader know that, perhaps, there can be ominous results from NOT knowing one's gun. The last two sentences not only confirm that, but also, and immediately, give the reader a glimpse at the bring-'em-on attitude he or she is about to encounter in the protagonist.

Carla Peltonen
Carla Peltonen and Molly Swanton, writing as Lynn Erickson
www.lynnerickson.com or www.marybalogh.com

The day it all began it was threatening to snow.

We started "Aspen" with this sentence to set the mood--a raw, upsetting scene that introduced our female protagonist and her troubled persona. It also coincides with winter in Aspen and skiing and the book's background. As a matter of fact, snow plays a big role in this book, softening the edges of reality at times and weighing on people, figuratively and literally at others.

The Hunter waited with infinite patience.

The Hunter in "Night Whispers" was the stalker, or rather, he was one of the stalker's multiple personalities. In the opening scene he was waiting for his victim, this time only to approach her, but his obsession grew throughout the book, and his infinite patience eventually paid off.

It started to drizzle a few minutes after the graveside service began.

Once again, we chose to open with a setting of the scene in "The Eleventh Hour." Our main character was attending the funeral of his murdered wife. The rain dripped tears from heaven, soaking everyone, lowering the sky claustrophobically, foreshadowing the unjust fate about to overtake the man, a fate as relentless as the rain itself.

Patricia Eakins
http://www.fabulara.com

When I think about story beginnings that do what they should do, I think of my story "Fertility Zone" (anthologized in *Vital Lines: Contemporary Fiction about Medicine*, Ed. Jon Mukand, 1990).

> **"'Harley...you know that dead woman?....That dead woman went and had her baby.'"**

There is a suggestion of forbidden knowledge--a suggestion of the gothic impossible. There is humor and irony in the earnestness of the voice. But the opening also does the sober work of hinting at themes of the story, which is about the relationship between a childless practical nurse and an anonymous traffic-accident victim, kept alive by a ventilator, who has given birth in this sub-comatose state. The nurse and her husband have lives that are barren in more ways than one, so "knowing" a dead woman when you see one--and what you know about her--is very much a notion that opens at the heart of the story.

Off the Shelf

Ryan was nearly killed twice in half an hour.
Tom Clancy, *Patriot Games*, 1987

I say in speeches that a plausible mission of artists is to make people appreciate being alive at least a little bit.
Kurt Vonnegut, *Timequake*, 1997

The day before Martin Burney lost his wife Sara he watched her walk away from him, her long hair lifted at the edges by wind from the Atlantic.
Nancy Price, *Sleeping with the Enemy*, 1987

Uptown traffic was terrible and there was an abandoned vehicle on the Henry Hudson Elway at Sixty-first Street that everybody was afraid to approach until the bomb squad got there.
Frederik Pohl, *The Siege of Eternity*, 1997

"My wife," John Wright said with a start, realizing he had lost track of her.
Andrew Coburn, *The Babysitter*, 1979

Once upon a time there were two cities within a city.
Ray Bradbury, *A Graveyard for Lunatics*, 1990

People's lives--their real lives, as opposed to their simple physical existences--begin at different times.
Steven King, *The Dark Half*, 1989

Across the tracks there was a different world.
Dorothy B. Hughes, *The Expendable Man*, 1963

Seventeen years old, and she couldn't remember murdering anyone, couldn't remember a trial or sentencing, or who, exactly, she had killed.
Scott MacKay, *Outpost*, 1998

The cold passed reluctantly from the earth and the retiring fogs revealed an army stretched out on the hills resting.
Stephen Crane, *The Red Badge of Courage*, 1952

The eyes behind the wide black rubber goggles were cold as flint.
Ian Fleming, *From a View to a Kill*, 1959

Danny Caiden was reasonably sure that there was nothing wrong with him.
James Blish, *ESPer*, 1952

She was so deeply imbedded in my consciousness that for the first year of school I seem to have believed that each of my teachers was my mother in disguise.
Philip Roth, *Portnoy's Complaint*, 1967

How unused, Carlotta pondered irresponsibly, Americans had become to crooked teeth in the young.
Cecily Crowe, *The Tower of Kilraven*, 1965

"I should feel sorrier," Raymond Horgan says.
Scott Turow, *Presumed Innocent*, 1987

It was news at the time.
L.P. Davies, *Genesis Two*, 1969

"Damn it, Frank. Where did you hide it?" Nell Pennington cursed, something she'd never do under normal circumstances. But then, her circumstances hadn't been normal since Frank Matson's heart gave out, leaving her at the mercy of a Louisville bank.
Patricia Waddell, *From the Heart*, 2000

It was morning, and the new sun sparkled gold across the ripples of a gentle sea.
Richard Bach, *Jonathan Livingston Seagull*, 1970

Duncan Makenzie was ten years old when he found the magic number.
Arthur C. Clarke, *Imperial Earth*, 1976

The parole officer came to the house on a hot Saturday afternoon in October.
John D. MacDonald, *The Price of Murder*, 1957

It was perfect.
Leonore Fleischer, *Rain Man*, 1989

A poor beauty finds more lovers than husbands.
George Herbert, *Jacula Prudentum*, 1651

Have you noticed the colors of the spines and covers?
Science fiction and mystery uses bright colors.
Horror spines are mostly black.
(And some collectors value SF simply for its cover art.)

6 -- Writer and Reader Interactions

Again, we have the author's promise to come through with a good read—whether this feat is set up through a shocking, subtle, or humorous opening. As Valerie J. Freireich says, "I try never to cheat my readers." Or as Charles L. Fontenay puts it, "story must assure the reader that it will not be a waste of his or her time to continue reading."

"The trick in writing a grabber opening is not just to get the reader excited; it's to make her curious. It's to make her want to know, 'What happens next? Why did the author start here?'" states Lawrence Watt-Evans.

Carolyn Wheat sums it up this way: "A compelling situation, an interesting turn of phrase, a provocative question are far better puller-inners than a lot of background information that just sits there."

Read on to learn what other experts say.

Insights

Joe Haldeman
http://www.sff.net/people/joe.haldeman/index.htp

I sometimes use classical "narrative hooks," but more often I move into a story in a more subtle way. My current novel, *Forever Free* starts with this line:

> **Winter is a long time coming on this god-forsaken planet, and it stays too long, too.**

-- which is not especially dramatic, but it's a line that resonates through the book.

I'm on the road right now, 2500 miles from my books, so I don't have a lot of examples to quote to you. The story "Odd Couplings" starts out with a hook of a kind:

> **The wind never stopped. It changed direction, sometimes disastrously, and the hurricane speed quieted to a gale sometimes, but it never stopped.**

It might be worth pointing out that sometimes you start writing a story because you've come up with an absolutely killer line -- and then by the time you've finished the story, you have to get rid of the line that inspired it.

Here are some examples I use in class, teaching "how to start a story:"

> **I wish to reveal a secret which I have carried with me nine years and which has become burdensome.** "A Burning Brand," Mark Twain

> **I do not think we ever knew his real name.** "Tennessee's Partner," Bret Harte

Sometimes the narrative hook would put you directly in medias res:

> **In walks these girls in nothing but bathing suits.** "A & P," John Updike

Or it might shock:

> **None of them knew the color of the sky. Their eyes glanced level, and were fastened upon the waves that swept toward them. These waves were the hue of slate, save for the tops, which were of foaming white, and all of them knew the colors of the sea.** (The Open Boat)

> **Not everybody knows how I killed old Philip Mathers, smashing his jaw in with my spade; but first it is better to speak of my friendship with John Divney because it was he who first knocked old Mathers down by giving him a great blow in the neck with a special bicycle pump which he manufactured himself out of a hollow iron bar.** (*The Third Policeman*, Flann O'Brien)

Again, more than a simple hook; hinting with its language at a strange kind of humor to follow.

Carolyn Wheat

My own favorite of my opener is:

> **'I thought she was dead.**

> **I hoped she was dead.'**

This is from *Troubled Waters*. What I hope it does is make readers want to know who 'she' is and why the narrator wants her dead and what will happen if she's not dead, which the next sentence will tell us she isn't. And, for those readers who already know the series detective, Cass Jameson, why is our knee-jerk liberal Cass wishing someone dead?

One thing I discover about opening passages is that the reader needs to know a whole lot less detail than beginning writers think. A compelling situation, an interesting turn of phrase, a provocative question are far better puller-inners than a lot of background information that just sits there.

Valerie J. Freireich

Shortly after learning he was married, Gray Bridger realized he might need to kill his wife.

This, the first sentence of my novel, *Testament*, is odd and intriguing but it is also true to the story. Offbeat, violent or enticing openings that have little or nothing to do with the plot or the theme of a novel are a form of authorial cheating; I try never to cheat my readers. It's a conceit of mine that I strive to open in a way that encapsulates the essence of a story. That Gray has to "learn" that he is married and to understand the need to kill his wife goes to Testament's heart.

How-to-write books sometimes state that a good method of opening is to grab readers by starting in the middle; I prefer to start at the beginning. Testament's action flows from Gray's discovery that he is married. In my first novel, *Becoming Human*, the first sentence is:

Alexander Greeneyes was hungry, but he wanted to live.

His hunger, a sign of his impending death, is the proximate cause of everything that follows. I'm of the opinion that if the genesis of a story isn't interesting, then perhaps there is a need to rethink the story.

Of course, I make concessions. The original first sentence of Impostor was: "In the beginning, life seems simple." I loved the juxtaposition of Genesis and the impression of cliché, but the sentence is part of a biology lecture given by the novel's main character, Marcer Brice, immediately before his arrest and exile.

To begin the story with the arrest would have created a more dramatic opening – the lecture goes on for two pages – but I really wanted that lecture in for thematic reasons. Instead of opening in either of those ways, and while attempting not to cheat the reader, I began Impostor with a point of view out of time sync with the rest of the novel, although the two timelines are brought into synchrony by novel's end.

To change timelines clearly, without confusing readers, I begin every chapter with a scene in the point of view of an unnamed "Supplicant." This new opening makes Marcer's lecture, which directly follows, more palatable because the Supplicant is asked, "Is Marc all right?" letting the reader know that however pedantic Marcer's lecture seems, something dangerous is about to happen to him.

Poul Anderson
http://www.poulanderson.com

The opening few words of a story are notoriously apt to be the hardest to compose. I am told that some writers put the task off till the body of the manuscript is completed. Certainly I spend a lot of time on mine, and often revise them over and over. There is no set rule. A vivid scene or turn of phrase is generally desirable, but sometimes the story is better introduced by something more quiet, perhaps even a little dry.

I think Tau Zero, a novel about a space voyage that lasts beyond the lifespan of this universe, starts as well as any I have done. This beginning amounts to four sentences in two paragraphs.

"'Look—there—rising over the Hand of God. Is it?'

'Yes, I think so. Our ship.'"

It's meant to convey a sense of epiphany. The degree of its success or failure is for readers to judge.

Charles L. Fontenay

I think my favourite opening of my own creation is that for a science fiction novel, *The Ghosts of Pembroke*:

Black he wore, all black, and death slumbered, waiting, in his hands and feet.

Leaning back against the oaken bar, Couguare Bataille balanced a tankard of sharp-sweet brew in his left

**hand, and surveyed the patronage in the tavern with
wary, sea-blue eyes.**

**His hair was wheat-gold, his shirt careless, open to the
drifting gaze...trousers slim and tucked in riding
boots...sword long at his hip, knife sheathed in wide,
loose belt.**

What you have in a story is a potential interaction between an
author and a reader. Intelligently, the author wants as many
readers as will to read his story, for both economic and status
reasons. The reader is not interested in the author "showing off" but
in a story whose reading will compete successfully with other
activities in personal satisfaction. Due to competition among
millions of stories available, the opening of the author" story must
assure the reader that it will not be a waste of his or her time to
continue reading.

It is very important for the author to be honest with the reader and
not advertise a story that is not the one that will be told. So the
opening must set the tone for the story. My old friend, Gordon
Dickson, told me once that he tries to capsule the entire story in the
opening—and I found that he succeeds in doing so. The opening of
mine that I have cited tells the reader that the story will be one of
violent action, and it is. The only thing I have omitted about the
story in this opening is that it depends as much on farcical humour
as on action.

A different kind of story requires a different opening tone. The
opening to one of my other novels, *Dionysos in Tears*, (contracted
but not yet published) shows that it is not an action story but one
devoted to inner emotional experience:

**As happens to us all, that season had come at last
when spring had fled into uncertain memory for John
Lion Deveron, its tantalizing hopes and prospects
fading to a wish. The golden-green of freshly awakened
foliage had darkened and clothed the lithe grace of
young limbs, the surprise of sudden sparkling showers
was suppressed with the approach of sedate summer.
The time of dreams had ended, ahead was only
maturing, the harvest, and ultimately the long cold.**

And yet...when all seems settled and staid, a laughing breeze may touch the cheek, a gentle mist may moisten the air and, miraculously, it is April again.

Lawrence Watt-Evans
http://www.sff.net/people/LWE/

People often have the wrong idea about the concept of the "grabber" opening sentence. The classic example I've heard cited several times is, "Bang! Bang! Bang! Three shots rang out, and I was off on the greatest adventure of my life."

I've heard that quoted a dozen times. The line sticks in my memory. But do I remember what it's from? No, I do not. Was it a classic work that everyone's read? No, it was not. Because, in fact, throwing the reader into the middle of the action like that is not necessarily the best way to hook him.

The trick in writing a grabber opening is not just to get the reader excited; it's to make her curious. It's to make her want to know, "What happens next? Why did the author start here?"
You don't need to start off with a bang, with something happening in your first sentence -- but you *do* want to start off with something intriguing.

I started my first novel, *The Lure of the Basilisk*, with:

"I am weary of all this death and dying."

The theory is that the reader will want to know who is tired of death, and what he's going to do about it – after all, what *can* anyone do about the inevitability of death?

Packing a lot of information into the first sentence can also pull the reader in. I began *The Cyborg and the Sorcerers* with:

He lay back on the acceleration couch and wondered idly whether he had been officially decommissioned, and whether anybody left alive had the authority to decommission him.

That suggests a great deal -- he's on an acceleration couch, which implies a spacecraft; he wonders not about discharge, which is how soldiers are released from service, but decommissioning, which is more appropriate to machines. And the question of who's left alive -- well, obviously there's some backstory here.

And sometimes just setting a scene, creating an appealing image, is enough -- in *The Wizard and the War Machine* I opened with:

> **Bright daylight spilled through the chunks of colored glass set into the windows, striping the fur carpets with bands of red and blue and green.**

That gives the reader a sense of the exotic, of barbaric luxury -- fur carpets, bright colors.

None of those try to hook the reader with raw action. Action is not what the "grabber" is about. It's the promise of something strange and exciting that catches the reader. It's not the reader's adrenaline that needs to be stirred; it's his curiosity.

Off the Shelf

As John Amalfi emerged on to the narrow, worn granite ledge with its gritty balustrade, his memory encountered one of those brief boggles over the meaning of a word which had once annoyed him constantly, like a bubble in an otherwise smoothly blown French horn solo.
James Blish, *Earthman, Come Home*, 1956

The trap had closed at sundown.
Poul Anderson, *Brain Wave*, 1954

At seven A.M., Allen Purcell, the forward-looking young president of the newest and most creative of the Research Agencies, lost a bedroom.
Philip K. Dick, *The Man Who Japed*, 1956

That morning, James Harker was not expecting anything unusual to happen.
Robert Silverberg, *Recalled to Life*, 1957

Arthur flung the stone with calculated aim.
Patricia Highsmith, *People Who Knock on the Door*, 1983

Every day since her husband's death, Dorrie Hunter Greene had learned something new and surprising about herself.
Claire Bocardo, *Maybe Later, Love*, 1992

Standing in front of his dresser mirror, the young man pointed the revolver at his reflection.
James W. Hall, *Under Cover of Daylight*, 1987

"It might be useful," said the rich, womanly voice, "to model me as your guardian angel."
Andrew M. Greeley, *Angel Fire*, 1988

She was a very old woman dressed entirely in black, and when she fumbled open my inner office door the aluminum tubing of the walker she was leaning on gleamed like nickel steel against the black of her dress.
Loren D. Estleman, *Sugar-Town*, 1984

A merry little surge of electricity piped by automatic alarm from the mood organ beside his bed awakened Rick Deckard.
Philip K. Dick, *Do Androids Dream of Electric Sheep?*, 1968 (Filmed as Bladerunner)

A rider passing out of the province from Mexico into the territory of Arizona encounters perhaps as white a terrain as can be found in any desert on earth.
Jay Hayden, *Sonora Pass*, 1970

Air-raid sirens were warbling the end of a practice alert when Bruce came through the train gate at Union Station.
Frank G. Slaughter, *Surgeon, U.S.A.*, 1966

Can you tell me, Octavia, why our luck never seems to change for the better?"
Colleen McCullough, *The Ladies of Missalonghi*, 1987

I was on my way to Mexico in the early summer of 1898, riding a good bay horse I called Drifter and leading an ignorant sorrel I called Feathers, partly because he was feather-legged but mostly because he was parrot-mouthed and birdbrained.
Sam Brown, *Devil's Rim*, 1998

For quite a few weeks now, Dan Willis had known he needed to begin a serious search for a job.
Frederic Bean, *Hard Luck*, 1992

Then there was the bad weather.
Ernest Hemingway, *A Moveable Feast*, 1960

I jerked upright in bed, clutched at my neck, and doubled over as a god-awful pain ripped through me.
Catherine Coulter, *The Edge*, 1999

She worked in one of those Park Avenue buildings which tourists feel obligated to photograph.
John D. MacDonald, *Nightmare in Pink*, 1965

**Old soldiers, sweethearts, are surest,
and old lovers are soundest.**
John Webster, *Westward Hoe*, 1607

Go west, young man, go west.
John L. Soule, *Terre Haute Express*, 1851

Insights

Eileen Kernaghan
www2.portal.ca/~lonewolf

The books I grew up with -- Hardy, Dickens, the Bronte sisters --were written in a leisurely era. Nineteenth century readers, more patient than nowadays, and more forgiving, were undaunted by stately beginnings and pages of description. I still love a novel that opens, like *The Return of the Native*:

A Saturday afternoon in November was approaching the time of twilight, and the vast tract of unenclosed

wild known as Egdon Heath embrowned itself moment by moment..." and so on for another three pages.

Today's readers -- especially young people -- come to a book with a different set of expectations. Something needs to happen quickly: in the first paragraph, or better yet, in the first sentence. That was the reality I had to face, when I began to write fantasy for the young adult market. My most recent book, *The Snow Queen* (Thistledown Press, Spring 2000) is loosely based on the Hans Christian Andersen fairy tale. It's a story that begins in an instant of transformation, when the heroine's safe, complacent world is abruptly turned inside out.

The fairy tale begins, in straightforward fashion:

> **Look you, we're going to begin. When we are the end of the story we shall know more than we do now....**

In what I hope is the same spirit, my version opens:

> **Looking back, years afterward, she thought she could name the day, the hour -- almost the exact moment -- when things began to go wrong.**

Mary Rosenblum
www.sff.net/people/MaryRosenblum

Fishing for Readers by Mary Rosenblum

Nita Montoya's brother sold her when she was fifteen -- to the Bee Man who came around sometimes to sell honey to the field hands.

That sentence opens my short story "The Bee Man," which appeared in the September 1991 issue of Asimov's Magazine. In that single sentence, I present the reader with several questions. When is this? Is this a slave system? Who is this Bee Man, and why did Nita's brother sell her? What's going on here? Some of those questions I proceed to answer rather immediately – the where are we, and when?

Others are not answered until the conclusion of the story -- they are the story.

We are a curious species, we primates. We are like Kipling's Elephant's Child, with our 'satiable curiosity'. We are happy when we can go and find out, and bored when we know all the answers. How many of you have finished a book once you discovered that you knew where the story was going, and knew how the characters would react to everything? To me, a story is a cascade of questions and answers that lead the reader effortlessly along, like a stone rolling down a hill. There are bumps and diversions, perhaps, but that downhill momentum is maintained throughout. And that all-important first paragraph is the shove that gets the stone rolling.

It is also called the hook. For a good reason. There are a lot of stories out there, trolling for the attention of our readers. Why read this one, and not the next one? We pick up a book, or leaf through a magazine, and we sample that first paragraph or two. If our curiosity is pricked sufficiently hard we turn the page, and we're caught. We buy the book. We buy the magazine. We read the story.

Questions and answers. As writers, we pose questions to our readers, and if we're skillful writers, we give them enough information to permit them to find the answers. Start with at least one question in that first sentence, or certainly in the first paragraph. Where/when are we? What is going on here? Why is this happening? Who are these people? The more questions that can be posed, the more the reader's curiosity insists that the all-important first page be turned. First paragraphs are like first impressions -- we form an instant opinion of the person or the story we have just met. We may modify that opinion if we pursue the relationship, but it is that first moment that entices us or sends us on our way.

Never tell the reader things that the reader does not need to know. The weather, our character's life history and appearance, the time of day -- these can all come along as needed. Unless they are a critical feature of the story, leave them out of that first paragraph. We all know the 'It was a dark and stormy night' cliche. If that 'dark and stormy' night provides a 'hook' that will entice our reader-fish, then by all means use it, but certainly write the sentence with more punch and authority!   The storm roared like a dragon...   The wind tore at the flimsy hut...

Another good example of an opening sentence comes from John Kessel's story. Every Angel is Terrifying: "Railroad watched Bobby Lee grab the grandmother's body under the armpits and drag her up the other side of the ditch." Where? When? Who? What is going on here?   These are the four questions that we should use to bait our story-hook. At least. Troll for those readers, and bait your hook well.   See how many questions we can pose to prick that Elephant's Child curiosity.

Martha C. Lawrence
http://www.marthalawrence.com

Below is some background about the opening lines from my first novel, *Murder in Scorpio*, which was nominated for the Edgar, Agatha and Anthony awards in 1996:

Fantastic as they may sound, the events in the Following narrative are true.

My name is Elizabeth Chase. I saw my first ghost when I was an undergraduate studying premed at Stanford.

I suppose that all fiction is a lie, in that authors 'make this stuff up,' as G.M. Ford says. Yet the sentence that opens my mystery series featuring psychic detective Dr. Elizabeth Chase in some ways is true. I did see a ghost when I was an undergraduate, and the paranormal events in the novel are based on my own real-life psychic experiences. There's power in truth, and savvy authors exploit that fact. Great authors have known for centuries that truth is stranger--and more compelling--than fabrication. They weave truth into their stories like strands of gold.

"You think you're going to get me, don't you? Well, you've got another think coming, 'cause I'm ready for you.

That's why there's a forged a card in my wallet saying my blood group is AB Negative, and a MedicAlert tag warning that I'm allergic to penicillin, aspirin, and phenylalanine. Another one states that I'm a practicing, devout Christian Scientist. All these tricks ought to slow you down when the time comes, as it's sure to, sometime soon.

Even if it makes the difference between living and dying, there's just no way I'll let anyone stick a transfusion needle into my arm. Anyway, I've got antibodies. So you just stay the hell away from me, ALAS. I won't be your patsy. I won't be your vector."
From the short story "The Giving Plague"

"I know, things taste better fresh, not packaged. Hamburger clots your arteries and hurts the rain forest. We should eat like our stone age ancestors, who dug roots, got lots of exercise, and always stayed a little hungry. So they say.
Still, I balked when my wife served me termites." From *NatuLife*

"...So you want to talk about flying saucers? I was afraid of that.

"This happens every damn time I'm blackmailed into babysitting you insomniacs, while Talkback Larry escapes to Bimini for a badly needed rest. I'm supposed to sit here in front of a mike and field call-in questions about astronomy and outer space for two weeks. You know, black holes and comets? But it seems we always have to spend the first night wrangling over puta UFOs." From *Those Eyes*

Point of view is difficult to establish in a story that's told in second person, present tense! I wanted a sense of immediacy, as if you're taking part in a realtime radio program... while diving right into the subject matter at hand.

> **"No one ever said it was easy to be a god, responsible for billions of sapient lives, having to listen to their dreams, anguished cries, and carping criticism.**
>
> **Try it for a while.**
>
> **It can get to be a drag, just like any other job."** From *Stones of Significance*

Now what needs to be said about that?

Most opening lines try to do several things at once. The must be intriguing. They should establish a point of view. And they should relate somewhat to the environment and circumstances that will be dealt with in the story. In *Glory Season*, I wanted to introduce the main character, establish her voice through a flashback, and show quickly (through dissonance in the calendar) that this is taking place on another world. It also sets the importance -- in the tale -- of distinguishing summer-born children from those born in winter.

G. David Nordley
http://www.sfwa.org/members/Nordley/

You present an interesting concept I suppose my best example of this genre was the opening paragraph of my SF mystery novella, "Network," (Analog, Feb, 1994) that went:

> **The severed head of a Kleth scientist, displayed with other evidence in a transparent case in the lobby of the presentation dome, set the mood for the gathering in the Trimusian Capital, Triapolis. Lieutenant Drinnil'ib of the Trimus Planet Monitors looked at it with forensic curiosity and over half a macroyear's experience. The eyes were unusually far apart, almost half a doci, for a Kleth, and the two notches in the Kleth's crest signified a warm weather birth; a congenital feature, if Drin**

remembered. A wonder of the universe that that tiny skull had contained a brain as powerful in life as his own. The plumage had been black, with the sun-bleached tips of a field worker, or avian athlete.

The beginning hook is probably not the most successful part of my writing, so I present what follows with this caution; please pay more attention to what I say about it than how well I execute.

I think many readers do make a decision about whether to continue reading or not in the first few paragraphs and that an author needs to provide a reason for them to keep reading. This is tricky in that readers are a varied group with a wide range of tastes and interests and a particularly strong statement in one direction or another may turn off as many as it turns on. Balance is important.

In the example above, I tried to provide a problem with a hint of danger in the context of a professional investigation, the immediate introduction of an otherworldly venue, and a context of realism and science rather than the supernatural.

So I see the problem as one of accomplishing several goals at once.

If you have a particular audience in mind, make sure that they understand that this is their kind of thing. I see merit in truth in advertising; I would much rather someone quietly turned to the next story than spend several hours with my story only to find out that what he thought was one thing was quite another and throw it across the room in frustration of time wasted. Oh, and remember that the most important person in that audience is the busy editor to whom you are submitting the work.

Also, there needs to be a problem, a question, or an event unresolved or not understood that can hook your readers' curiosity to the extent that they are willing to pursue it through a few paragraphs necessarily heavy in the background of character and setting. It may not be the main course, but it should at least keep your readers around long enough to get a whiff of what's to come.

Finally, there are those who care not a whit about what is written as long as it is written well (whatever "well" means to them), so that first paragraph should probably be written as "well" as you can write anything. But write it in your own voice, of course, for there is no accounting for taste and that voice is what you will sustain.

Off the Shelf

The winter before he was sixteen, Pup sold his soul to the devil.
Ruth Rendell, *The Killing Doll*, 1984

Maybe returning to New York on the day after he left it had been a mistake.
Poul Anderson, *The Shield of Time*, 1990

When I picked up the mail at the post office, I found one first-class envelope in with the usual junk.
Phyllis A. Whitney, *Daughter of the Stars*, 1994

It grieved me to leave you, considering how mad you were.
Patricia Anthony, *Flanders*, 1998

Buck did not read the newspapers, or he would have known that trouble was brewing, not alone for himself, but for every tidewater dog, strong of muscle and with warm, long hair, from Puget Sound to San Diego.
Jack London, *The Call of the Wild*

As the stupid, piggy Chevrolet Impala floated through buzzard-infested desert, Isadore "the Mensch" Goldman was thinking that he was slightly surprised there really was a *state* of Nevada.
James Patterson, *Season of the Machete*, 1997

Something unpleasant was going to happen, something incredibly and overwhelmingly unpleasant. John J. Malone was sure of it.
Craig Rice, *Knocked for a Loop*, 1957

She felt the snake between her breasts, felt him there, and loved him there, coiled, the deep tumescent S held rigid, ready to strike.
Harry Crews, *A Feast of Snakes*, 1976

"Never write a novel in the first person," Jack told me.
Donald E. Westlake, *A Likely Story*, 1984

The soft purr of the turbine was almost lost in the roar of wind as the gray sedan traveled south through the New Mexico night.
John D. MacDonald, *Wine of the Dreamers*, 1951

Brick Gordon's mood was evil, his temper short, and he was well aware of it.
Lynn Westland, *Thunder to the West*, 1964

Never mind what they tell you on Madison Avenue.
Max Shulman, *Anyone Got a Match?*, 1964

I lay without moving in the low, narrow crawl space under the front porch of our home near West Point. My face was pressed tightly against the brutally cold, frozen ground littered with dry leaves and scratchy brambles. I knew I was going to die soon, and so was my baby girl. The word from a song, Crosby, Stills, and Nash—"Our house is a very, very, very, fine house"--played in my mind.
James Patterson, *Hide & Seek*, 1996

I was a child molester.
Joyce Carol Oates, *Expensive People*, 1968

Janet Jeppson Asimov

"Artificial intelligence is an abomination!" The shout came from the gallery and was instantly hushed, but not before the biofundamentalist delegates nodded in agreement. (*Mind Transfer*)

At the time I wrote this, I was horrified by religious fundamentalism's battle against the scientific view of the universe. I extrapolated that battle into the future, when there might be sophisticated robot brains—opposed by "biofundmentalists" regardless of the fact that human minds could live longer by transfer into such brains.

I hoped that my two opening sentences would let the reader know instantly what could happen.

Now, ten years later, I'm even more horrified.

M. K. Wren /Martha Kay Renfroe

http://mkwren.com

This adage, attributed to Cecil B. DeMille, the producer of epic films, is a favorite of mine:

"Begin with an earthquake and work up from there."

For hooks, that works, if you lean hard on the word UP.

In general, I think what readers want in a hook is something that sets the tone for the story, gives them a foretaste of the characters and/or setting, and promises that something interesting is happening or is about to happen. It's not often a writer can get all that into a sentence or so, but we need ideals.

My first (published) hook opened *Curiosity Didn't Kill the Cat*, in which Conan Flagg, Oregon's first resident, series-character detective, made his debut. The hook took the form of a radio announcement:

> **". . . according to Coast Guard spokesmen at the Holliday Bay Station, gale warnings have already been posted. Residents are warned to expect 50- to 70-mile-per-hour winds, with occasional higher gusts. . . ."**

Well, dark and stormy nights may not be the most original hooks, but at least the impending storm is something interesting about to happen, and in this hook I managed to hint at the setting, even if I didn't get to any characters. And stormy weather is important in this story at the climax.

One hook that I intentionally thought about as a hook--and it's perhaps a little self-conscious as a result--is from the Conan Flagg mystery, *A Multitude of Sins*:

> **Meg stretched herself, obliterating most of Harney and Malheur Counties in a gray fog, then she smiled her**
>
> **Mona Lisa smile, blue jewel eyes half closed, and challenged him to do something about it.**

This is what I call a double-take hook. It doesn't quite make sense at first, and the writer hopes the reader will keep on reading to find out what's really going on. In the next paragraph or so, it becomes clear, of course, that Meg is a blue-point Siamese (a recurring character in the Conan Flagg series, but what's an old bookshop without a cat?) and that the geography she's obliterating is a map in a book Conan is studying.

Too cute? Maybe. That's a risk I take whenever I write about animal characters, especially when it's based on a real animal. In this case, the original was Tai, the doyenne of the old Lincoln Book Shop in Nelscott, Oregon. She was a regal lady who believed in noblesse oblige, and she was more famous than most of us will ever be. When she died—at the age of twenty--she had a two-column obituary, complete with a photograph, in the largest newspaper in the state.

I think my best hook was in my mainstream novel *A Gift Upon the Shore*:

I will call it the Chronicle of Rachel.

A simple little thing, but it has a lot going for it. (For one thing, I liked its meter.) It establishes the first-person narrative, introduces the central character, and suggests, with the word Chronicle that this will be a history covering many years. The word will suggests something that hasn't happened yet, but is going to be important.

But I have to admit that when I began writing the first draft of *Gift*, I wasn't thinking about an enticing hook. That just seemed the logical place to begin, with that declaration of intent about the Chronicle, which is so vital to the story.

And, finally, here's the opening paragraph of *Neely Jones: The Medusa Pool* (1999).

Blood red and night black, chrome flashing like a biker's chains, the big, customized pickup rumbles north, headlights sweeping vacant asphalt. At this hour--nearly midnight--the pickup encounters no traffic in Westport, except a semi heading south.

Time and place is established, and there's a sense that something bad is about to happen--anybody who drives a rig like that is up to no good--but the overriding concern here is setting the tone of the story; the mood. Neely Jones is a new series character, an African-American woman in a small, hopelessly white-bread town. She was the only non-white, non-male deputy in the county sheriff's department--its token black and token female in one--but now she's the sheriff, and all the deputies are just waiting for her to take one false step. Her first testing is a murder case—and the victim is her lover of five years. I wanted to suggest in the hook a feeling of menace, of a powerful threat impervious to reason and incapable of mercy.

By the way, for Conan Flagg fans, he's just on sabbatical. And since he and Neely live in the same county, I wouldn't be at all surprised if they ended up working on a case together someday.

Off the Shelf

There are some men who enter a woman's life and screw it up forever. Joseph Morelli did this to me—not forever, but periodically.
Janet Evanovich, *One for the Money*, 1994

At first Officer Jim Chee had felt foolish sitting on the roof of the house of some total stranger.
Tony Hillerman, *Sacred Clowns*, 1993

My decision to become a lawyer was irrevocably sealed when I realized my father hated the legal profession.
John Grisham, *The Rainmaker*, 1995

The Right Honourable Zadkill F. Obomi could feel the weight of the night pressing on his grey-wire scalp like the oppressive bulky silence of a sensory deprivation tank.
John Brunner, *Stand on Zanzibar*, 1968

It was like he was doing me a favor taking me to this place.
Judith Rossner, *Looking for Mr. Goodbar*, 1975

When the power went I was finishing a ten-page report.
Sara Paretsky, *Tunnel Vision*, 1994

The drought had lasted now for ten million years, and the reign of
the terrible lizards had long since ended.
Arthur C. Clarke, *2001: A Space Odyssey*, 1968

I am an old man now, but then I was already past my prime when
Arthur was crowned King.
Mary Stewart, *The Crystal Cave*, 1970

The main entrance to Falconer--the only entrance for convicts,
their visitors, and the staff--was crowned by an escutcheon
representing Liberty, Justice and, between the two, the sovereign
power of government.
John Cheever, *Falconer*, 1975

Inside the windowless courtroom, a man awaited sentencing for
murder.
Nancy Taylor Rosenberg, *Mitigating Circumstances*, 1993

When at last they found her and took her out of the water I knew I
had to go down and look at her.
John D. MacDonald, *All These Condemned*, 1954

Captain Inish Scull liked to boast that he had never been thwarted
in pursuit—as he liked to put it—of a felonious foe, whether
Spanish, savage, or white.
Larry McMurtry, *Comanche Moon*, 1997

Time is not a line but a dimension, like the dimensions of space.
Margaret Atwood, *Cat's Eye*

"Why did I do it?" asked Golan Tervize.
Isaac Asimov, *Foundation and Earth*, 1986

The last class of my old professor's life took place once a week in
his house, by a window in the study where he could watch a
small hibiscus plant shed its pink leaves. The class met on
Tuesdays. It began after breakfast. The subject was The Meaning
of Life. It was taught from experience.
Mitch Albom, *Tuesdays with Morrie*, 1997

I never knew my mother.
Sheri S. Tepper, *Beauty*, 1991

7 – What about Action?

Years ago authors could ease into a story. Personally, I am a mystery addict and the thing I most like about American authors is that you get plopped right into the story. No sneaking up on it. Blam. Conflict. Who? What? When? Where? Why? We arrive just in time. The story has begun.

On the last day of school, after walking to the old brownstone building on 85th where they had an apartment, Peter's father told him that they would be going away for a few months.
Greg Bear, *Dinosaur Summer*, 1998

Everyone agreed was the grandest and most beautiful wedding in Palm Beach history, but nearly everybody also felt that something was terribly, dreadfully wrong.
Pat Booth, *Palm Beach*, 1985

On the desk in my candlelit study, the telephone rang, and I knew that a terrible change was coming.
Dean Koontz, *Fear Nothing*, 1998

Some urgency exists and must be solved NOW. But, as stories go, it's not that simple. The urgency gets your attention, but the resolution comes about 200 pages later.

Insights

Sarah Smith
www.sarahsmith.com

Neil Gaiman tells a story about himself as a small boy.   He and a friend both read fantasy constantly, and one day the friend confided that, when he grew up, he wanted to be a writer. Gaiman considered this. Finally, thoughtfully, he said, "I want to be a wolf."

Writers want to be wolves. Detectives. Heroes. Villains. We want to experience the Other. We want to get outside ourselves, to find out what's out there, beyond the bag of skin and perception in which we find ourselves. We want to find the universes behind other eyes.

In the first paragraph, introduce the wolf.

> **The Baron Alexander von Reisden went mad after his young wife died, and in five years he had not got himself sane. His friends were concerned about him. He had tried suicide, once, early on, and had not succeeded; this was encouraging in a man who was usually both well-prepared and lucky; but even mad, Reisden might reasonably have assumed that he could shoot himself through the heart without missing, and, knowing himself, at the first moment he could, he would have learned how to do it better. He still had the gun...**

Here is a wolf: a man who doesn't think like you and me.   He's controlled, but in an odd way: he "might reasonably have assumed that he could shoot himself through the heart without missing..." He's intelligent and competent; he has friends; but they don't sound useful to him now. He has to fix whatever has happened to him himself (why does he think that?), but he can't depend on himself. And he has the gun.

He's going to make a very odd detective.

The Vanished Child was my first historical novel, and because I was nervous, I must have written about 284 versions of this paragraph in which I made it abundantly clear that this story, dear reader, was happening in 1906. Every one of them was wrong, of course. The story isn't about what year the book was in; its about the man, this wolf of a man, who can't save himself, who has to find what has driven him mad before it kills him.

Claire Delacroix
Claire Cross; Château Delacroix
http://www.delacroix.net

The pace of our world is getting faster by the moment, its focus shifting to rapid visual images, and this as a result of technological change. The Internet, video games, computer software, television and movies all directly reflect these developments, but the fallout can also be felt in fiction, particularly commercial fiction.

Simply put, we are tougher to entertain. And books, being a non-image-based technology are at an obvious disadvantage.

This means that fiction must be tighter, description must be immediately relevant, dialogue must sparkle and conflicts must be more sharply drawn. Nowhere is this more necessary than in the opening paragraphs of a book. The reader must be engaged, snared by the characters or the conflict, right from the first few paragraphs of the book. The author must hit the ground running - and the best way to do this is to find the event that sets the story in motion and begin right in the thick of it.

Added to that are the issues of specific genres. Romance is an emotional genre, in that it is critical for the reader to emotionally bond with the characters. A successful romance encourages the reader to sympathize with the heroine and fall in love with the hero. To this end, I like to introduce one or the other protagonist first, give the reader some insight into character by letting that character respond to the story's conflict. Then I bring hero and heroine together within the first chapter, ideally as a direct result of the first character's doings.

In *My Lady's Desire*, the reader meets the hero first:

> **Yves stepped into the blessedly private shadows of his silk tent and deliberately ignored the cheers of the crowds. They were chanting his name, but Yves had no intention of returning to the fields again.**
> **Ye gods, but he hated tourneys.**

The hero is immediately established as a champion, yet a man who places little value in his success. The point here is to intrigue the reader, to make her wonder what kind of a man Yves is - - and what he thinks is important. By the end of the first scene, Yves will be granted an offer that should be impossible to refuse - but the stage is set for him to defy expectation. His refusal leads to the heroine repeating the same offer - when he accepts her terms, the reader knows why.

As a technical aside, the first scene is written in Yves' point of view, so the reader understands how he thinks. When the heroine Gabrielle appears, that scene is written from her point of view. In this way, the initial meet of the hero and heroine is richer for the reader, letting the reader share in both perspectives and giving her insight into both characters. The tool encourages the emotional bond between reader and characters which is so critical for romance.

In *The Princess*, the reader meets the heroine first:

> **Tullymullagh could not be lost!**
>
> **Brianna ran down the corridor, blind to the intricate tapestries hanging on every wall and indifferent to the wondrously fitted stones of her sire's creation. She tripped over her full skirts, cursed with a vehemence that would have made her father scowl, then gathered her embroidered hems by the fistful and ran on.**

Again, character is revealed first. The reader is faced with an indulged, impetuous heroine, one whose family's wealth (and her way of life) is at stake. Note that clues to the heroine's character are interwoven with the description of her home, making the sentences work on two levels. From this opening, the reader can easily guess that Brianna will not simply stand aside and watch her world be destroyed. That leaves the question of what she will do, particularly when faced with a marriage arranged to cement the conquest of her home. Her bold demand for a choice is perfectly in character - and brings the hero Luc into the story.

Valerie Wolzien
http://www.nmomysteries.com/main.htm

I think my very best opening line is in my first mystery, *Murder at the PTA Luncheon.* The line is

Nothing is worse than having a nice sex fantasy interrupted by the memory of a murder.

And I wrote it not to get the attention of someone browsing through the shelves at Barnes and Noble but to get the attention of an editor. I had been told that editors read scores of manuscripts every month and that they only paid attention to the ones with `sexy' first pages. I took that advice literally and had my main character lying by the swimming pool dreaming of a sexy lover when she remembers the murder of a friend.

I've written sixteen books since that time and that's the only one where sex has been mentioned in the first line.

Robert Chase

As I get more serious about this business, I find myself paying closer attention to my peers and my betters. For a writer accused of verbosity, nothing can beat the single line opening of Dickens' "A Christmas Carol:"

Marley was dead, to begin with.

How intriguing, and vaguely disturbing, those last three words. If you can extend that drive for two or three pages, like James Lee Burke does at the beginning of *Cimmarron Rose,* you cannot only hook the reader, you can sound all the themes of the coming story as effectively as the overture to a Romantic opera.

For the SF writer, it helps if the opening establishes that this is definitely a science fiction or fantasy story. A couple of my stories have received favorable comments in that regard. From *The Game of Fox and Lion*:

> **Crashing down the quantum ladder, splashing out a halo of Cerenkov radiation, the Gryffon's Pride fell into normal space.**

Throw the readers into the action immediately, while letting them know that the book in their hands is, at least in part, a fast-moving space opera. Or, to hold attention through a necessary data dump, this more terse opening to *Shatter the Sky*:

> **It was a bad day, even before the robot tried to kill him.**

A hook, though necessary (or at least highly desirable) is not sufficient. An editor who specifically noted that he loved the opening of *Shatter the Sky*, nonetheless declined to buy it even though, IMHO, it is a more interesting and mature work than, say *The Game of Fox and Lion*. One must still endure the vagaries of publishing.

Off the Shelf

My family hated my job.
Susan Isaacs, *Close Relations*, 1980

"The work is, you understand, somewhat unusual," said Mr. Gordon.
Poul Anderson, *The Guardians of Time*, 1960

I finished making the third bomb a few minutes ago.
Bill Pronzini, *Booby Trap*, 1998

The hospital was exactly like any other hospital--green and white and hygienic and profoundly depressing under a veneer of brisk jollity.
Patricia Moyes, *Death and the Dutch Uncle*, 1968

The gravestones were black.
Elizabeth Peters, *Legend in Green Velvet*, 1976

Theoretically a policeman, like a priest, should be above politics, or at least untouched by party politics, yet it is the policeman who is responsible for enforcing the laws made by the politicians.
J.J. Marric, *Gideon's Vote*, 1964

It was a hot June day when I discovered my father's secret, which was to change the whole course of my life as well as his.
Victoria Holt, *The Demon Lover*, 1982

The hours while other people sleep are the longest for me, and the most uneasy.
Marcia Muller, *While Other People Sleep*, 1998

Anyone who has ever dealt with the common cow will readily swear that he beast by far surpasses all other four-legged animals and most two-legged in the race for the title of the most miserable critter the Good Lord ever created.
Kent Conwell, *Panhandle Gold*, 1991

The sky above the port was the color of television, tuned to a dead channel.
William Gibson, *Neuromancer*, 1984

Eleanor stood before the abbess' oak table, hiding her fear behind the deceptively sweet smile and innocent expression she always assumed in the presence of Authority.
Ellen Jones, *Beloved Enemy*, 1994

On the day of my husband's annual fund-raising gala, I was down by the river liberating rats.
Ann Rivers Siddons, *Fault Lines*, 1995

On the first morning of her husband's lingering death, Lucy Todhunter one day came down to breakfast alone.
Sharyn McCrumb, *If I'd Killed Him When I Met Him*, 1995

Most of the time I stayed clear of towns, preferring my own company and that of some animals to most people, but there are times when I enjoy getting to see some lights and to hear some noises I haven't made myself.
Frank Roderus, *Sheepherding Man*, 1980

Steven Womack
http://www.womackbooks.com

Every writer searches for an opening line that will immediately grab a reader and pull him or her directly into the story. An opening line that positions the reader in respect to the story is an added bonus to an effective opening lead. Most of my books have been written in the first-person point of view, so in addition to the first two purposes of an effective story opening, I also try to immediately create a compelling and attractive voice for the narrator.

One particularly effective strategy I've used is to have my protagonist immediately say something that cannot help but get a reader's attention. For instance, in my novel *Chain of Fools*, which is a fairly dark novel set in the world of adult "entertainment," I have my narrator Harry James Denton begin the book by saying:

"Don't get me wrong; I like sex."

This immediately positions the audience. The reader knows, or senses, that this is a story about sex and that it takes a peculiar perspective on the subject. Why else would a narrator have to defend what he's about to say?

At the other end of the spectrum, in my novel *Way Past Dead*, which is a convoluted and at times absurd story involving a cult that seizes control of a morgue by surrounding it in armed Winnebagos, I decided that the opening sentence of the novel should set the scene by being as convoluted and absurd as the story itself. The result is the longest opening sentence I've ever gotten away with:

The night the fundamentalist redneck zealots assaulted the morgue, I was hauling butt down I-65 from Louisville back to Nashville after spending three days lying in the grass videotaping a disabled, wheelchair-bound bricklayer shooting hoops on his brother-in-law's patio.

From my experience, the only thing harder to come up with than a really effective, dynamite opening line is an equally powerful title. But it's all part of the process, and an awful lot of fun.

Joan Hall Hovey
http://www.angelfire.com/ca3/joanhallhovey

I try to draw the reader into my story by engaging his or her senses. For example, if my story takes place by the ocean then I want my reader to smell the kelp, hear the waves pounding the rocks, feel the salt spray on his/her face. To quote E.L. Doctorow: 'Good writing is supposed to evoke sensation in the reader — not the fact that it's raining, but the feel of being rained upon".

I want, though, to do more than that in those first couple of paragraphs. (Which is as much as many editors will read before rejecting a book.) I will introduce a main character and involve him or her in some action. Suggest conflict.

In my novel, *Nowhere to Hide,* I wanted to place the reader in that dark, narrow space where the killer was, to have him feel something of what the killer felt. To give a sense of the evil that existed within him. To do that, I, myself, must first get inside the killer's skin, as an actor must crawl inside the skin of a character he is playing, if he is to be convincing.

> **The closet door was at the top of the stairs at the end of the hall. To get to it he had to pass by two doors, one on either side, both now partly open. He could hear talking, very low. Farther away, the sound of running away. In three quick strides he was past the doors and inside the closet. He knew he was smiling.**

> **He felt excited the way he always did when he got past them. Even if anyone had got a glimpse of him, it wouldn't really matter. He was invisible. The invisible man.** (*Nowhere to Hide*)

So began what I intended to be a nail-biting read. Reader's comments and heart-warming reviews have told me that I succeeded.

Having said all of the above, my new book begins with a sentence that simply came to me: (No doubt after a lot of work from the subconscious, which Stephen King calls, 'the boys in the basement'. I'm paraphrasing, but that's close.) I don't know if the following sentence will remain in the book, but here it is anyway:

The first time I saw the house I knew it didn't want me.

That sentence intrigued me. I wanted to know more. It seemed to me that readers would, too.

Alan Dean Foster

When I decided I wanted to write an entire novel from the point of view of an alien, I was looking for a way to immediately establish in the mind of the reader the alienness of the principal protagonist, while at the same time rendering it (in this case a "him") familiar enough so as not to scare the reader off. By definition, any truly alien alien would be incomprehensible to a human...which would reader a book unreadable. A little gentle levity can also make otherwise stark alienness easier to take. And simultaneously, you want to intrigue the reader into reading on.

Hence the opening line of my first contact novel, *Nor Crystal Tears*.

It's hard to be a larva.

Off the Shelf

It was Jobbo first told me about the car snatches.
Ed McBain, *Big Man*, 1959

When he finally did make love to Greta Garbo, she wore a glove.
Ben Greer, *Time Loves a Hero*, 1986

Elizabeth had just turned sixteen when she saw the plantation for the first time.
Julian Green, *The Distant Lands*, 1991

I accepted a commission that had been turned down by four other writers, but I hungry at the time.
Dick Francis, *Longshot*, 1990

The place was cheap and dirty and smelled bad, just about the scurviest-looking dive Jeff Meyer had ever seen in his twenty-one years, and he had seen plenty of them lately.
Alan E. Nourse, *The Mercy Men*, 1955

It crawled along the hell-black ocean floor, searching with its five large dark eyes.
Piers Anthony and Clifford A. Pickover, *Spider Legs*, 1998

The first thing she did upon arising was count her money.
Gene Wolfe, *Counting Cats in Zanzibar*, 1996

The morning her mother rose from the dead, Samantha Adams stood out in her driveway loading up her car, nothing more on her mind than heading for Atlanta to sing "Happy Seventy-Fifth" to her uncle George.
Sarah Shankman, *Digging Up Momma*, 1998

Towns, like people, have souls.
Rita Mae Brown & Sneaky Pie Brown, *Murder on the Prowl*, 1998

I know from Lucy's voice that she is scared.
Patricia Cornwell, *The Last Precinct*, 2000

People who didn't know her thought Miranda was aloof.
Gwen Davis, *Silk Lady*, 1986

The bastard looked dead.
Peresa Medeiros, *Heather and Velvet*, 1991

Brian Herbert
http://www.dunenovels.com/

When I first started writing novels in the 1980s, I was told that I needed to hook an editor in the first three pages of my manuscript. Today, in our microwave, instant-gratification society, we probably need to hook that editor—and the reader—on the very first page. This makes the narrative hook even more essential than ever before.

With co-author Kevin J. Anderson, in the *House Atreides*, the first of three DUNE prequels to be published by Bantam. Our opening lines in this novel are:

> **Lean and muscular, Baron Vladimir Harkonnen hunched forward next to the ornithopter pilot. He peered with spider-black eyes through the pitted windowplaz, smelling the ever-present grit and sand of this place.**

Lean and muscular? But in Frank Herbert's classic science fiction novel *Dune* he established that the Baron was so fat and weak-legged that he couldn't walk without the aid of suspeensors, with which he floated in the air. The reader is thus hooked by *House Atreides*, and has to read more in order to find out how the Baron became debilitated before the later events of *Dune* unfolded.

My father's opening for *Dune* is extremely provocative. In an epigraph he mentions an unidentified person, Muad'Dib, who has spent his first fifteen on the planet Caladan, but then develops an eternal attachment to Arrakis—the planet known as Dune. Dad then opens the narrative with this sentence:

> **In the week before their departure to Arrakis, when all the final scurrying about had reached a nearly unbearable frenzy, an old crone came to visit the mother of the boy, Paul.**

The reader is left with many intriguing questions. Who is the exotic-sounding Muad'Dib, and is this the same person as Paul? If they are the same, why does he, like Dune, have two names? Who is the old crone and why is she interested in the boy? An air of mystery pervades the opening of the novel.

In *God Emperor of Dune*, Frank Herbert opens with:

> **The three people running northward through moon shadows in the Forbidden Forest were strung out along almost half a kilometer. The last runner in the line ran less than a hundred meters ahead of the pursuing D-wolves. The animals could be heard yelping and panting in their eagerness, the way they do when they have the prey in sight.**

The reader is made to wonder who these unfortunate people are, what the (apparently ferocious) D-wolves are, and what the Forbidden Forest is. The more questions the author can suggest, the better, just as long as the reader isn't irritated by complexity.

In the prologue of my first novel, *Sidney's Comet*, I set a scenario in which garbage that Earth has catapulted into deep space is coming back, in the form of an immense garbage comet. The reader is left wondering what events led to this potential catastrophe. In the first epigraph of another novel, *Prisoners of Arionn*, I describe in technical detail how a group of aliens has sliced away a chunk of Earth (including the San Francisco Bay Area), has enclosed it all in a space habitat, and has stolen it away into deep space, without harming the inhabitants. The novel then centers on a dysfunctional family that is aboard the purloined fragment. In *The Race for God*, I open with the revelation that the God of the Universe has contacted an unlikely religious charlatan, instructing him to deliver a message. That startling message, the reader soon learns, is that God has provided the exact celestial coordinates of His location in a distant galaxy, and has invited humans to come and visit Him.

Successful narrative hooks refer succinctly to momentous events that are already in progress as the story begins, and the reader must turn pages in order to find out what has caused the present state of affairs.

My neighbor, David Guterson, began his Faulkner award-winning *Snow Falling on Cedars* with:

> **The accused man, Kabuo Miyamoto, sat proudly upright with a rigid grace, his palms placed softly on the defendant's table—the posture of a man who has detached himself insofar as this is possible at his own trial.**

Instantly the reader wants to know more about this proud man whose Japanese name and demeanor are so intriguing.

B. A. Chepaitis
http://www.fearprinciple.com/

I think one of my favorite openers is from the third novel in the series featuring Jaguar Addams, *Learning Fear*. (*The Fear Principle*, and *The Fear of God*, are the first two.)
Learning Fear starts with the sentence:

The man on Jaguar's bed was thoroughly naked, and fully erect.

I thought it was an intriguing opening, especially since the place it leads to is not where you might expect. In this novel, Jaguar ends up as an academic in a university, trying to behave herself among the people of the ivory tower. Since Jaguars aren't domesticated animals, it doesn't quite work out. But you might have guessed that from the opening sentence.

Mark L. Van Name

Opening lines are the side-show barkers of fiction, imploring readers to come on in and sit down for the show. Exactly how they do that is the writer's choice, of course, but almost by definition they must do one thing: Offer the reader something interesting. I don't believe any formula applies in all situations, and I sure don't have a formula I use with openings. I do, though, like openers that mix a bit of emotion with a bit of mystery, as in the following from the story "Basic Training" (in the Baen Books anthology *Armageddon*, 1998):

I knew I wasn't supposed to look anywhere but straight ahead, but I wanted to check down the road to my right, to see if Mom was still there. After she dropped me off everything happened so fast that I didn't even know if she had left yet or if she was still watching me. I sorta wanted her to watch me, but I sorta didn't, because she had started crying when the men yelled at me to get in line, and that had made me feel like crying and I knew I shouldn't cry. Daddy taught me that. Men don't cry. Now that he was gone I was supposed to be the man.

The reader here learns that the narrator is a young boy who has lost his father and is in a tough situation. To find out exactly what that situation is, the reader must keep going—the whole point of the opener.

I don't like to dive into a story until I have the opening right, though I often end up revising it after I've finished the piece.

Off the Shelf

To have a reason to get up in the morning, it is necessary to possess a guiding principle.
Judith Guest, *Ordinary People*, 1976

Nancy Greeney lay on the operating table on her back, staring up at the large kettle-drum shaped lights in operating room number 8, trying to be calm.
Robin Cook, *Coma*, 1977

I awoke on my knees, bound to the bed and spattered with blood from the IV tubes I had pulled free.
Alfred Coppel, *Wars and Winters*, 1993

The first bullet hit Matthew Hope in the left shoulder.
Ed McBain, *There was a Little Girl*, 1994

As often as humanly possible, he tried to put Suzanne out of his mind.
Mary Higgins Clark, *Let Me Call You Sweetheart*, 1995

One day the sky fell.
Kim Stanley Robinson, *Green Mars*, 1994

The train was an hour late reaching Bridge, California, but this was not bad because some days it did not get there at all.
John Reese, *Sure-Shot Shapiro*, 1968

Jenny began looking for the cabin at dawn.
Mary Higgins Clark, *A Cry in the Night*, 1982

I am a robot.
Isaac Asimov, *Gold*, 1995

Once there was a dead man.
Larry Niven, *A World Out of Time*, 1973

The crow with the red eyes sat on a branch in the towering old white oak where the leafy boughs were thickest and stared down at the people gathered for their picnic in the sunny clearing below.
Terry Brooks, *Witches Brew*, 1995

There is no substitute for talent.
Aldous Huxley, *Point Counter Point*, 1928

**Nothing spoils a romance so much as
a sense of humour in the woman.**
Oscar Wilde, *A Woman of No Importance*, 1893

**All history, so far as it is not supported by
contemporary evidence, is romance.**
Samuel Johnson in Boswell's *Tour to the Hebrides*, 1936

Where the Sleuths Live

Mystery authors writing a series often place their characters (detectives, homicide investigators, salvage consultant, coroner, and so on) on the perimeters of our continent. Sleuths are concentrated in Boston, New York, Virginia, Florida, Louisiana, California, and Washington.

8 -- Interest Yourself and Your Reader

Writers like to amuse, fascinate, and outdo themselves. The only way to succeed in anything is to do your best. The only road to performing your best is to keep yourself fascinated with the work.

True, authors on assignment may have to be self-starters. But writers who write about what they want have the greatest opportunity to become addicted to the topic, and just perhaps, take the editor, then the public, by storm.

Knowledge is the edge. The Writers' Golden Rule is "write about what you know." True. Combine that with red-hot enthusiasm and you've got a deal!

Insights

Jennifer Blake
http://www.jenniferblake.com

One of my favorite books on writing is a guide published almost 50 years ago, *How to Write a Novel* by Manuel Komroff. This was my introduction to the idea of hooking the reader, and I still use its basic recommendations. Komroff said "Every good beginning should have movement and promise." I suppose today we might be more likely to use the words "action and intrigue," but the premise is probably more important now than it was back in 1950, before the attention span of the average reader was shortened by exposure to the fast pace of television.

In *Kane*, a contemporary romantic suspense tale with a plot that involves shenanigans in the funeral industry, the lines are:

> **Regina Dalton snapped awake the instant the coffin lid closed.**
>
> **Darkness pressed around her like a smothering blanket. Not a sliver of light penetrated. The dense air smelled of old dust and ancient velvet. The side walls seemed to contract, so she was supremely aware of her left shoulder wedged against padded wood while her right nestled beneath unyielding solid flesh and bone.**
>
> **Warm flesh and bone.**

To come up with this scene, I started out by making a list of everything I could think of with any connection to funerals. One of the items on my list was, of course, "coffins." This word triggered a memory of something I'd read about the great 19th century actress, Sarah Bernhardt, keeping a coffin in her parlor and receiving guests while reclining in it. I'd once seen a photo of her in this famous casket with her face framed in lace and with a calla lily clasped in her hands. The leap from that image to putting my main character in a coffin was instantaneous. After that, it was just a matter of playing, "What if . . ." I'm not sure what this says about how a writer's mind operates to create hooks, but there it is.

Several things make this scenario work. First is the instant plunge into dramatic action: the main character is shut up, alive, in a coffin. Horror is inherent here because this is an ancient fear shared by the general population. Then a puzzle is presented because it's an old coffin rather than a pristine modern casket. From a craft point of view, the ploy gets the story off on the right foot by acting as a lead-in to the story setting. But the real kicker is in the intrigue factor, since the heroine is not alone in her place of entrapment.

The incident begs several immediate questions: Who put Regina in the coffin? Why? Where is this coffin? Why is it old? Is she being buried alive? Is the person lying against her newly dead or still living? Is it a man or a woman and why is he or she there? And, most important, how on earth is Regina going to get out?

The value of any hook can be judged by the number of questions it creates in the mind of the reader. The challenge, then, is to see how much action and intrigue can be crammed onto the first page. Coming up with good hooks is one of the most important parts of being a writer, but also one that's most fun. I usually feel I've succeeded when my latest idea makes me grin with diabolical enjoyment and jump-starts my own interest so I can't wait to write the rest of the story.

Phyllis Ann Karr

I remember a Perry Mason movie in which Perry proves the culprit cannot be the true author of the manuscript. That provided the motive for murder because he is unable to quote its opening paragraph verbatim. Perry says something like, "Every writer I know tells me it's impossible to forget a book's beginning words, because whose are the ones he's worked hardest to perfect." Well, sir, this test proves that I haven't written any of my own novels and short stories!

Except, maybe, two. My favorite prose opening is from *The Downstairs Apartment*, my attempt at an almost quasi-autobiographical "supernatural scare" novel, which never found a publisher. The manuscript is at my mother's house seventy miles away, and I have forgotten my hero's last name and exact age, but the first paragraph runs more or less thus, and seems to me to encapsulate the hero's character very nicely. (Incidentally, Leslie is not the character I based on myself.)

> **At age thirty-six, Leslie Fairchild had been looking for himself for eighteen years. Sometimes he was afraid he had found himself.**

The other one hardly counts, because it's in Tennysonian blank verse, mostly composed whilst I took my daily walks:

> **The lady Guenevere, who once was queen,**
> **And ruled all Britain with a gracious hand**

> **Beside her lord, lived now a cloistered nun;**
> **Her days a round of prayer and work and prayer**
> **Her nights a narrow cot, and memories,**
> **Alone, unlighted, in her narrow cell.**

Thus begins "An Idyll of the Grail," one of the works I'd most like to be remembered by, published in Mike Ashley's 1996 anthology *The Chronicles of the Holy Grail*.

It isn't that I fail to lavish plenty of thought, labor, care, and revision, on my openings. I lavish all that on every page of my fiction. Often, however, the key passages (to my own way of thinking)—the ones I keep going back to and tinkering with months after the work is provisionally finished—occur somewhere near the middle. To choose one example: I had to chop about 26,000 words out of *Frostflower and Windbourne* in less than a week. On the whole, I think the shortened version a much better book; but there is one passage that I should dearly love the chance to reinstate. It would have come on page 86 of the published edition: while witting outside the farmer-priests' holy hall enjoying the beauty of the hymn, *Frostflower* muses in wonder that these singers are the same people she once heard shouting for her blood. I had totally forgotten the novel's first paragraph, even though, on looking it up, I considered citing it for my favorite published opening.

I finally settled, however, on the start of the novel I would probably have been proudest of had the text not gotten so badly mutilated in the editorial department, *Wildraith's Last Battle* (1982):

> **At about the time Gilmar the Old entered the war**
> **between Senerthan of the Long Forest and Dulanis**
> **Butter-hair, a widow who lived beyond what was then**
> **the farthest reach of the fighting lost her child to the**
> **god of the woodlands...**

This introduces the reader right off the bat to the novel's two intermingling themes: the huge armed conflict raging throughout almost the whole known world of the setting, and the very small, personal, one-on-one grievance of a bereaved mother for a deity. It promises large-scale action, human interest, and theological leavening—about as much as I've ever managed to pack into so few words.

Openings seem to me only part of a much larger picture. I'm really more concerned with such points as drawing up my cast of characters, choosing the viewpoint, and figuring out the timetable of events. Somebody has said, "Start writing, and then throw out the first two pages." It isn't bad advice—I occasionally follow it—but it suggest that what the author finds most grabbing isn't necessarily what will grab the reader; and this brings me to my last point:

Perhaps one of the most important functions of the narrative hook is one I've never seen mentioned: Before you worry about hooking the reader, you have to hook yourself—the writer—into your own story.

Sheila Finch
http://home1.gte.net/web10g3j/index.htm

My favorite opening line was written for my first published novel (though not the first written), *Infinity's Web*.

She would never forgive herself for not being there when her son was born.

The novel explores the alternate world's theory of quantummechanics, and what it means in the life of one woman, Anastasia Valerie Stein. The traumatic experience of blacking out at the moment of her child's birth is heightened by his subsequent death. These "absences" become increasingly problematic for her; she's often inexplicably "not there" when she should be, causing family upheavals and making her fear for her sanity. This prompts her to begin a search for explanations for the tantalizing glimpses she gets of other versions of her life.

It seems to me that the first line is a key to the novel. Unfortunately, my publisher, Bantam, didn't think so. They wanted to reverse the order of the first two chapters of the novel because they felt my second chapter (about one of Ann's rather bizarre alter egos) was more exciting. As a new author, I didn't feel I had the power to insist on my version. So as a result, my favorite first line isn't after all.

Off the Shelf

They were old hundred-dollar bills, a little limp now, even a little greasy, and one of them had a rip in it that somebody had neatly mended with a strip of Scotch tape.
Ross Thomas, *The Porkchoppers*, 1972

In Devon's dream they were searching the reservoir again for Robert.
Margaret Millar, *Beyond this Point are Monsters*, 1970

Everyone had always said that John would be a preacher when he grew up, just like his father.
James Baldwin, *Go Tell it On the Mountain*, 1952

He was an old man who fished alone in a skiff in the Gulf Stream and he had gone eighty-four days now without taking a fish.
Ernest Hemingway, *The Old Man and the Sea*, 1952

The desk at the Grand Hotel in Bombay was crowded with incoming guests.
Pearl S. Buck, *Come My Beloved*, 1953

The wind had died.
Raymond E. Feist, *Shards of a Broken Crown*, 1998

At the time of Professor Beatrice Sterling's arraignment, she had never set foot in a criminal court.
Amanda Cross, *Murder Without a Text*

He could not get used to going to the girl's apartment.
Elmore Leonard, *52 Pick-up*, 1974

If it had been up to Katie Chave she would have called in sick that morning.
Lillian O'Donnell, *No Business Being a Cop*, 1979

For some of us, of course, nothing would be enough.
Nancy Kress, *Beggars and Choosers*, 1994

Angela Ricci wished again she had a dog.
Carlene Thompson, *In the Event of My Death*, 1999

Like a cradle, the hearse rocked him gently.
Jeffery Deaver, *Praying for Sleep*, 1994

"Here's the truth of it...I can have any woman I want any time I want. No problem. Every one of them is ripe and ready, waiting to hear the magic words that'll persuade them to do anything. Married, single, older, younger, desperate, widowed, frigid, horny,...point 'em out, and they're mine."
Jackie Collins, *Thrill*, 1998

Elizabeth Boleyn, who an hour ago had been Elizabeth Howard, shifted her weight from one knee to the other.
Mollie Hardwick, *Blood Royal*, 1988

The old woman--80 if she's a day--distorts perspective, throws off scale.
Susan Dodd, *Mamaw*, 1988

Reading someone else's e-mail is a quiet, clean enterprise. There is no pitter-pattering around the room, no opening and closing the desk drawers, no percussive creasing as you draw the paper from the envelope and unfold it. There is no sound but the melody of the dial-up, the purity of the following Gregorian tones, and the sweet nihilistic measure of static. The brief elemental vibration that means contact. And then nothing. No smudge of ink, no greasy thumbprint left behind. In and out of the files, no trace. It could be the work of a ghost, this electronic eavesdropping.
Jane Hamilton, *Disobedience*, 2000

Why Walter woke up earlier than usual on August 10, Saturday, he couldn't at first explain.
Jane Hamilton, *The Short History of a Prince*, 1998

Sixteen light years from Earth today, in the fifth month of the voyage, and the silken force of nospace acceleration continues to drive the starship's velocity ever higher.
Robert Silverberg, *Starborne*, 1996

All around them the cacophony of greed carried on in its most glorious and extreme excess. But it couldn't make a dent in their world.
Michael Connelly, *Void Moon*, 2000

It was calm and starry at 20,000 feet.
Mike Cogan, *Top Gun*, 1986

When an explosion takes place lots of bits and pieces fly all over the scenery.
Eric Frank Russell, *The Great Explosion*, 1962

"I have to do it the same way every time," the woman said, her voice full and steady even though she was deep into her workout on a stationary bike.
Andrew Vachss, *False Allegations*, 1996

By the time they truck us to the staging area, which is the parking lot of some old church, the train has been burning for two days.
Nancy Kress, *Maximum Light*, 1998

Genius is one-percent inspiration and ninety-nine percent perspiration.

Thomas Alva Edison, *Life*, 1932

Murder Bone by Bone,
Lora Roberts
http://www.NMOMysteries.com

Through the window over the diaper table, in the back yard, I could see them hitting.

I tried to hurry with diapering Moira, but she kept squirming away from me, chattering loudly in a language known only to herself. I let her stand up, but then I stuck her ever so slightly with the diaper pin. I should have used the disposable diapers. Bridget had gotten a supply of them before leaving me with her four interesting offspring for a week.

I had spurned the disposable diapers on the grounds that they were not ecologically sound. I was going to be supersitter. I was going to have everything under control. I'd been in charge for a total of two hours, fifteen minutes, and already it was disintegrating all over the place.

Bloodthirsty screams came from the back yard. Framed in the window, I saw Corky, the seven-year old, whack his next brother Sam with what looked like a big bone. I blinked, but the weapons didn't change. Sam, five, also armed with a bone, hollered with outrage and swung back. Mick, the three-year old, dug placidly in the sandbox. While I watched, he used a reddish-brown curve of cranium to scoop up some sand. He picked something out of the sand he'd scooped and regarded it thoughtfully before popping it into his mouth.

I grabbed Moira's small, damp palm and hurried her out of the room. Two hours, twenty minutes, and counting. It was going to be a long week. (fourth Liz Sullivan novel, *Murder Bone by Bone*)

The hook is supposed to get a reader interested in your book from the opening page, and keep her/him involved in reading further. For me, it serves the same purpose for the writer. An interesting opening sentence, wherever it comes from, keeps me as a writer pursuing the story, finding out what it means. This opening has the advantage of including several of my own favorite themes as a reader—old bones, children, domesticity gone awry. When I'm enjoying the writing process, everything goes more smoothly. I really enjoyed writing this book, and part of that is because I had a great time following this hook into the narrative.

I don't know what alchemy transmuted the opening scene from *The Sound and the Fury* into the opening scene in my book. All I know is, when I pictured this scene, the boys in the back yard whacking each other with human leg bones, Liz in the house seeing this as just one more (to her) mystery of child-rearing, it all came together. I paraphrased Falkner (hope he doesn't mind, and come back to pound me with his own desiccated femur) because that conveyed the sense of immediacy I was looking for, the feeling you get when you read *The Sound and the Fury* of a narrator who is overwhelmed by visual stimuli. I wanted the reader to feel that sense of immersion. Also, I wanted the reader to have a great deal of sympathy for Liz, who represents beleaguered parenthood here. Anyone who's ever tried to keep up with small children will want to go deeper into the story to see if she succeeds in doing so.

An added bonus for this opening was the fun I had reading it at bookstore events. I hadn't thought about that before, but believe me, I'm thinking of it when writing hooks for future books.

Joe R. Lansdale
http://www.joerlansdale.com/

The opening sentence or paragraph may not be the most important thing in a novel as a whole—that would be every line from first to last—but it is hard to dispute that the first sentence or paragraph is the deciding factor for most readers when they are making the decision to put their money down and enter into the world of the author. A dull opening may in fact keep a book on the shelves. I, for one, nearly always open a book I'm considering purchasing, and read the first sentence or two, sometimes the first several pages if the opening sentence hooks me, I assume a lot of readers are like me.

For this reason, I believe, though it is not necessary to blow the world up in the opening, it is necessary to excite, or intrigue, or surprise, horrify, or humor the reader from the beginning.

My method is to think of one reader only. Me. I'm the only one I know anything about. I can't judge other readers, as we all differ. But I assume if the opening appeals to me, there's a good chance it will appeal to others.

I'm going to be immodest here and present some of my own openings, just as if I didn't know that article or not, this is a great opportunity to introduce readers to my books. Also, I have a certain idea about what it was I was trying to accomplish with these openings.

> **I'm writing now about the time before things got weird
> and there was high school to kiss off, college to plan,
> girls, parties, and the All Night Horror Show come
> Friday night at The Orbit Drive-In off I-45, the largest
> drive-in in Texas. The world, for that matter, though I
> doubt there are that many of them in, say, Yugoslavia.**
> (*The Drive-In*)

That's a couple of sentences, but I like to think it sets an air of mystery, and a dollop of nostalgia.

> **I was out back of the house in the big field with my
> good friend Leonard Pine the afternoon it started. Me
> with the twelve gauge and him pulling the birds.**
> (*Savage Season*)

This one is more subtle, but already you know a lot about the narrator. He's not fancy, he's acquainted with guns, and his best friend is a guy named Leonard Pine. What I think works best here is the straightforward tone and a subtle feel of trouble brewing, although trouble is not mentioned at all. The narrator, Hap Collins, merely mentions that it was "...the afternoon it started." If I did my job, this should be slyly ominous. You want to know what it is, and you have a feeling it isn't good.

> **That night, Ann heard the noise first.** (*Cold in July*)

Simple, but one of my favorites of my own openings. This pulls the reader right in. What noise? And if it's night, a noise is even more important. What's out there? What's going on? Is it dangerous?

> **When I got over to Leonard's Christmas Eve night, he
> had the Kentucky Headhunters turned way up over at
> his place, and they were singing "The Ballad of Davy
> Crockett," and Leonard, in a kind of Christmas
> celebration, was burning the house down next door.**
> (*The Two Bear Mambo*)

This one, another Hap and Leonard book like *Savage Season*, lets you know that the narrator is somewhat droll, primarily because it's obvious he's dealt with this kind of thing before. He knows Leonard well, and the narrator has a sense of humor. We know a little about

Leonard by the music he listens to. Hot country, and the tune is about an American hero known for his honesty and courage and folksy expressions. This applies to both the narrator and Leonard. And, I like to believe, the reader will want to know why Leonard is burning that house down. Again.

> **It was mid-April when I got home from the offshore rig and discovered my good friend Leonard Pine had lost his job bouncing drunks at the Hot Cat Club because, in a moment of anger, when he had a bad ass on ground out back of the place, he'd flopped his tool and pissed on the rowdy's head.** (*Bad Chili*)

Hap and Leonard again. Darkly humorous opening. We know that Leonard has a temper and that he can be dangerous, and that he works tough jobs. Since he's a bouncer, we have some idea of his economic status, and the tone of this opening, if I've done my job, lets the reader know they are in for a ride.

> **Wild Bill Hickok, some years after he was dead, came to Mud Creek for a shoot out of sorts.**
>
> **I was there. Let me tell you about it.** (*The Magic Wagon*)

One of my favorites of my own books. This one is an offbeat Western. We establish the Western tone immediately with the mention of Wild Bill Hickok, a Wild West icon, and we set a tone of mystery and intrigue with the comment abut the shootout taking place after Hickok's death. And, we have a comfortable narrator anxious to tell us the story. We're invited in.

Final word. Every sentence in a book has to be given the same effort, but the opening is the most important. A book is like a door and the opening is like a key. That key either works or it does not. If it doesn't, the reader puts the book down, if it works, he uses that key to open the door that leads into the room of your story. It's as basic and obvious as that.

Off the Shelf

The microphone was shoved into her face.
Catherine Coulter, *False Pretenses*, 1988

When Edward Carney said good-bye to his wife, Percey, he never thought it would be the last time he'd see her.
Jeffery Deaver, *The Coffin Dancer*, 1998

It was almost impossible to get to Lexington and Sixty-third Street.
Danielle Steel, *Fine Things*, 1987

"Will they see us?" she whispered.
Jonathan Gash, *The Grace in Older Women*, 1995

Ryder opened his tired eyelids and reached for the telephone without enthusiasm.
Alistair MacLean, *Goodbye California*, 1977

A bright flash of insight, to match that peculiar sun...
Roger Zelazny, *The Hand of Oberon*, 1976

Early in the spring of 1750, in the village of Juffure, four days upriver from the coast of The Gambia, West Africa, a manchild was born to Omoro and Binta Kinte.
Alex Haley, *Roots*, 1974

The first severity of mourning was over.
G.M.T. Parsons, *Laura*, 1978

Mr. van Haagen glanced about the table at Gad's and said benevolently, meaning well, "It is not often that one has the happiness of seeing so many old faces after so few years."
Norah Lofts, *The Haunting of Gad' Hell*, 1979

Whenever he rode into this town--which was every other week or so to report the condition of John Isely's scattered cattle holdings--Will Bonner was sure the place had grown since last time.
Dwight Bennett, *The Cheyenne Encounter*, 1976

The train stopped here for exactly two minutes, and by the time Leatherman had swung down off the Pullman and taken his suitcase from the porter, the whistle blasted and it was on its way again.
Richard Meade, *Cartridge Creek*, 1973

Frank Thompson

I never give first sentences a second thought.

Or, to put it another way, I obsess over them endlessly.

To me, the opening has to contain a little charge, something either powerful enough, or inexplicable enough, to keep the reader slogging through the rest of the piece, no matter what subsequent obstacles the writer may fling in the way. The writer has a paragraph or two -- at most -- to fully engage readers' interest, but the opening is the moment when you grab them by the lapels, back them into a corner and compel them to listen to what you have to say.

I do, however, waffle on this point somewhat; it all depends on what I'm writing, and in what style. In my books I don't feel an overwhelming need to whip the reader to attention; I figure we both have time to settle in and warm up to one another. I look at books as a progression, a journey from point to point, something that begins here and ends there.

Articles, on the other hand, strike me as being more circular in form. I like to bang in with something pithy and engaging as a kind of clue to what's coming, then work my way around the track until I can end at the beginning, offering a final thought that relates directly to the first -- a punch line to the opening "knock knock." I spend far more time thinking about opening lines in articles than in books.

I wrote an article upon the death of silent film star Lillian Gish some years ago and I opened it this way:

Lillian Gish once kissed me on the Phil Donahue Show.

The line seemed to be kind of a grabber -- almost any reader would be at least marginally curious as to how this odd event came to pass. After writing a few hundred words of appreciation about her life and career, I paid off the opening by explaining that I had once written a song about Lillian and presented it to her from the audience of the Donahue show, whereupon she invited me to the stage and kissed me on the cheek. I then ended the article with a few lines from my song.

None of my books starts with a grabber like that -- they usually ease into their subjects with the kind of sleepy, unconcerned leisure that, to my wife and others, defines my personality at its liveliest.

There is one exception, kind of, and to explain it, I must give away a little secret that I've never really talked about with anyone. That secret is, I always include one joke, or play on words, in my writing that only I will understand. Even my worst enemies concede that I have a sense of humor all my own--and that doesn't imply good *or* bad—and it tickles me a little to work in an odd line or to connect words or thoughts in a way that will at least make sense to the reader, but which will be funny only to me. Confused? Good; we'll continue.

I started doing this at the very beginning, got the idea to do this while writing my very first book, a critical biography of film director William A. Wellman. This book, by the way, was the very first thing I *ever* wrote -- no articles, no nothing – so I was literally learning how to write a book by writing a book. Wellman's first film was released in 1923 and called "The Man Who Won." I thought there was a kind of symmetry in containing the title of this first film in the first line in the first chapter of my first book. And so the chapter begins:

**The man who won the heart and hand of Celia
Guinness McCarthy was perhaps her least likely suitor.**

This sentence isn't a grabber, particularly, although I think it's a graceful enough way to start a chapter. But as a first sentence goes, it's one of my favorites, simply because it had extra meaning only (up until now) to me.

Off the Shelf

The map under glass made no sense.
Nicholas Jose, *Avenue of Eternal Peace*, 1991

Late in August three crows took up residence in the chimney of the corner house on Hemlock Street.
Alice Hoffman, *Seventh Heaven*, 1990

I'm as peaceful a man as you're likely to meet in America now, but this is about a death I may have caused.
Reynolds Price, *The Tongues of Angels*, 1990

Quentin Fears never told his parents the last thing his sister Lizzy said to him before they pulled the plug on her and let her die.
Orson Scott Card, *Treasure Box*, 1996

There are no prizes for guessing almost right.
Gerald Hammond, *Whose Dog Are You?*, 1991

Alex slammed the door as hard as she could, the sound venting some of her irritation.
Phyllis A. Whitney, *The Ebony Swan*, 1992

She sits in the corner, trying to draw air out of a room, which seemed to have plenty just a few minutes ago and now seems to have none.
Stephen King, *Rose Madder*, 1995

Tom Sanders never intended to be late for work on Monday, June 15.
Michael Crichton, *Disclosure*, 1993

A time came when my wife and my law partners were convinced I was going crazy and the best I could reply was "I hope not."
Clifford Irving, *Final Argument*, 1993

There was a university somewhere in the Midwest, Jack had once heard on the radio, which had an instrument package designed to go inside a tornado.
Tom Clancy, *Debt of Honor*, 1994

North of Appalachia an outcropping of wilderness survived.
Piers Anthony, *Omnivore*, 1968

That last stretch of forty-odd miles was the worst of the entire trip.
Howard Browne, *Thin Air*, 1953

There was no getting around it. Edna Ellett had picked an impossible week to die.
Sara Hoskinson Frommer, *Buried in Quilts*, 1994

They found her in the trash.
Julie Garwood, *For the Roses*, 1995

In the week before their departure to Arrakis, when all the final scurrying about had reached a nearly unbearable frenzy, an old crone came to visit the mother of the boy, Paul.
Frank Herbert, *Dune*, 1965

For one whole year he did nothing but drive, traveling back and forth across America as he waited for the money to run out.
Paul Auster, *The Music of Chance*, 1990

The first time I laid eyes on Terry Lennox he was drunk in a Rolls-Royce Silver Wraith outside the terrace of The Dancers.
Raymond Chandler, *The Long Goodbye*, 1953

Julian Morell's enemies often said he could never quite make up his mind whom he loved more, his mother or himself.
Penny Vincenzi, *Old Sins*, 1989

"What is taking so bloody long in there!"
Bent over the swollen and struggling body, the midwife shifted her eyes momentarily to the door. Yet even the dreadful shadows and thick pitted wood which separated them could not keep his terrible venom from stinging sharply. Nothing could.
Jaclyn Reding, *White Heather*, 1997

Mystery Authors' Pseudonyms

Some of these mystery authors write under more than one pseudonym.

Pseudonym	Author Name
A.A. Fair	Erle Stanley Gardner
Josephine Tey	Mrs. Zenith Jones Brown
David Frome	Elizabeth MacKintosh
Hugh Pentecost	Donald Westlake
Ed McBain	Evan Hunter
Oliver Bleeck	Ross Thomas
George Orwell	Eric Blair
John LeCarre	David John Moore Cornwell
Barbara Vine	Ruth Rendell
Carr or Carter Dickson	John Dickson Carr
Ross Macdonald	Kenneth Millar
Dell Shannon; Lesley Egan	Elizabeth Linington
Patricia Wentworth	Dora Amy Dillon Turnbull & Mary Violet Heberden
Thomas Costain	Pat Hand
Leslie Charteris	Leslie Charles Bowyer Yin
William Haggard	Richard Clayton
Edgar Box	Gore Vidal
Sara Woods	Sara Hutton Bowen-Judd
Michael Collins	Dennis Lynds
Brett Halliday	Dennis Lynds
Catherine Aird	Kinn Hamilton McIntosh
Tucker Coe; Richard Stark	Donald Westlake
Mickey Spillane	Frank Morrison Spillane
William Arden	Dennis Lynds
Charles L. Leonard	David Dresser

9 -- Prologues and Epilogues

An author may use a prologue independent of an epilogue; an epilogue sans prologue; or, frequently, both. In a novel, the prologue allows the author to separate him- or herself from the work and speak directly to the reader. Called "back-story," this material is the author's chance to fill in any details and add bits of history that may not be revealed in the story itself.

Used as flashback, flashforward, or simply background, the writer can suspend time, providing a transition so the reader expects chapter 1 to begin at a different place or time.

An epilogue is merely a "wrap-up" for the author or a conclusion from the narrator or main character. It may be in the form of a list of characters, indicating what happened to them. Sue Grafton, Carl Hiaasen, Mary Jo Putney, Fern Michaels, and Aileen Schumacher often use this technique. The technique is especially useful when it ties into the prologue.

Rarely does a reader not find the answers to all his questions in by the outcome.

Insights

Fern Michaels
http://www.fernmichaels.com

I've been writing for 27 years and during those years I don't think I ever gave a conscious thought to using a hook to open a particular book. If anything, I would say I shied away from using such a device. I much prefer writing a three-page prologue or a three-page opening chapter and grabbing the reader with either the last paragraph or the last sentence. When a prologue isn't called for, I write a short chapter and do the same thing. This gives the reader a little bit of an edge. I'm one of those people who will stand in a book store and read those three pages. I've also read the hooks and then skimmed to see if those hooks are going to enhance the story. Most times, they don't. That's my opinion.

I would like to give you this example. I just turned in a book titled "The Guest List" where I did a three page prologue that set the scene for the entire book. In three pages I showed a husband and father standing in the doorway of his wife's hospital room after she delivered a baby daughter and used his introspect to show what kind of a person he is and the level of his anxiety at that particular moment. In another descriptive paragraph, I showed how the wife and new mother was 'arranged' in the bed along with a few choice words of dialogue to show the reader what kind of person she was. The husband's best friend appears which allows for more dialogue to explain the husband's anxiety over the fact that his new daughter was not a boy as the wife hoped for along with the fact that the child was born with a Port-wine stain that covered half her face. Page three ends with the following words from the wife and new mother. "Are you telling me I gave birth to a freak?"

This one closing sentence sets the tone for the whole book. To me, the closing sentence is more important than an opening hook, which most times doesn't do justice to the rest of the text. It works for me.

Jane Toombs
http://www.alpine.net/~toombs/

If I use a prologue, which I do sparingly, it's because the story seems to require one. I don't use it for back-story, but for the purpose of setting up a problem the characters will be forced to solve in the book,
plus a foreshadowing and the chance to begin a circle that will close in the epilogue. An example from one of my books:

> **1947: Phoenix James strode across green fields toward the hill. Culloden House lay behind her. She'd left the man she loved more than anything else in the world. Had she left him forever?**

This is the opening of the prologue in my historical saga, *The Scots* (1984), a book that ranges from 1820 to 1947. The hook is obvious, but the prologue is also a foreshadowing of how Phoenix's Scottish ancestors were forced to flee from Scotland to America, leaving everything behind as Chapter 1 begins in 1820. The epilogue, in 1947 again, circles back to the hill Phoenix climbs, answers the question posed in the prologue, and offers a brighter future for the Logan clan.

Another reason for the use of a prologue is to set a mood, as this illustration from one of my serial killer books shows:

> **They'd forgotten to leave his door ajar again, so he lay in darkness. His heart pounded in fear; the dark wasn't his friend. And he sensed evil.**

From *Then Came the Darkness* by "Ellen Jamison," published in 1992: In this story, though there's no epilogue, the final chapter circles back to the disabled boy, who is finally safe and who's frightening mind link with the killer has helped to capture this evil man.

When a prologue isn't necessary, which is more times than not, the hook that entices the reader in the first chapter can also incorporate snippets of information. In this opening from my current contemporary romance, a Silhouette Special Edition, *Designated Daddy*, the hero's name is mentioned, his occupation is hinted at and book's location is established:

> The Capital Beltway evening traffic was no worse than usual, but to Steve Henderson, who was coming off a tough case, coping with the rush of cars and trucks edged his tiredness into exhaustion. The strident buzz of his agency beeper was the last straw.

Kate Freiman
http://www.poboxes.com/kate_freiman

This is the opening to *Lady Moonlight*, a romantic fantasy:

St. Helena, Napa Valley, California, Monday, May 24, 1999

The package from Ireland came by courier just after eight in the morning. His first impulse was to drop it into the trash and pretend he never saw it, but he knew that wouldn't work. Instead, after setting it on the counter, he ignored it and ground beans for a pot of coffee. While the coffee maker sputtered, he drank a glass of orange juice, then showered. When he came back to the kitchen, he studied the package from a short distance, simultaneously curious and wary. It looked harmless, but his gut warned him that anything with his grandfather's return address could be as volatile as a letter bomb. A glance at the microwave oven clock told him he only had time for breakfast before he had to meet his partner in San Francisco.

Without conscious intent, Con fingered the talisman suspended on the thin gold chain around his neck.

The strategic choice writers face for the opening of a story is: hit the ground running, or start in the ordinary world of the protagonist? Because *Lady Moonlight* is a romantic fantasy, I decided to start in the protagonist's ordinary world (a term used by Joseph Campbell and Christopher Vogler in describing a hero's mythic journey), just as it's about to change.

Originally, I'd written the opening from the point of view of the heroine, Aisling, but created the prologue from the hero's perspective to assure the reader that even though the story begins in 1899, it's indeed a contemporary story, while simultaneously teasing the reader to wonder how two people a century apart can be romantically connected.

By showing Con using his morning routine to deliberately ignore the "call to adventure" represented by the package from Ireland, I convey his reluctance to accept the as yet unknown challenge. The references to time are intended to alert the reader that time will be a major player in the story. And the image of this reluctant hero absentmindedly fingering a "talisman" signals the likelihood that some kind of magic is afoot.

Off the Shelf

I spotted Merlin Gilly standing against the empty space where the Hotel LaSalle had stood two minutes earlier.
Loren Estleman, *The Hours of the Virgin*, 1999

We didn't know we were an odd family.
Caroline Bridgwood, *Trepasses*, 1988

The 727 was lost in a sea of cumulus clouds that tossed the plane around like a giant silver feather.
Sidney Sheldon, *The Stars Shine Down*, 1992

In 1980, a year after my wife leapt to her death from the Silas Pearlman Bridge in Charleston, South Carolina, I moved to Italy to begin life anew, taking our small daughter with me.
Pat Conroy, *Beach Music*, 1995

It came by regular mail in a cheap white envelope that could have been purchased at any dime store.
Helen Nielsen, *Seven Days Before Dying*, 1956

The crowd of reporters outside the house in Bel Air parted to let the hearse through.
Michael Korda, *Queenie*, 1985

Cursing as his horse stumbled and went to its knees Dan Ragan kicked free of the stirrups and leaped clear of his saddle.
Ray Hogan, *Ragan's Law*, 1980

The one room stone jail was pierced by a single small high window.
Dave E. Olson, *Lazlo's Strike*, 1983

There were three of them, although sometimes there was only one of them.
Clifford D. Simak, *Shakespeare's Planet*, 1976

When Ellen Wainwright was married to Richard Lancy in July, 1873, the day was so hot that the church doors were left wide open, and towards the end of the ceremony, a stray dog ran in and stood howling in the central aisle.
Mary E. Pearce, *Cast a Long Shadow*, 1977

The sea which lies before me as I write glows rather than sparkles in the bland May sunshine.
Iris Murdock, *The Sea, The Sea*, 1978

You could always blame it on the heat...
Wade Miller, *Kitten with a Whip*, 1959

When she was quite sure that Willie was dead Zanny began to scream.
B.M. Gill, *Nursery Crimes*, 1986

It was a lie, but it was not a lie that could do any damage.
Rosie Thomas, *All My Sins Remembered*, 1991

She sometimes thought that for her, Nancy Chamberlain, the most straightforward or innocent occupation was doomed to become, inevitably, fraught with tedious complication.
Rosamunde Pilcher, *The Shell Seekers*, 1987

If this is such a gol'dang good idea, how's come we're hiding it from the grown-ups?
Stephen Calder, *Bonanza: The Ponderosa Empire*, 1992

Amerigo Bonasera sat in New York Criminal Court Number 3 and waited for justice; vengeance on the men who had so cruelly hurt his daughter, who had tried to dishonor her.
Mario Puzo, *The Godfather*, 1969

The boss was dying.
Erich Segal, *Prizes*, 1995

In these days cheap apartments were almost impossible to find in Manhattan, so I had to move to Brooklyn.
William Styron, *Sophie's Choice*, 1976

"The patient died about twenty past midnight," the night nurse said.
Jonathan Gash, *Prey Dancing*, 1998

Aileen Schumacher
http://www.aliken.com/aileen/

I KNOW that opening sentences are supposed to grab the reader from the outset, that their main purpose is purportedly to prevent the reader from putting the book down. But while I am aware of this goal, my opening sentences in my prologues (we'll just skip the discussion of how books with prologues don't sell!) are always chosen with an eye for their counterpart in the epilogue.

I am an engineer, and I write a series with an engineer protagonist, so that probably contributes to my need to have some sort of thematic closure in the books I write. But beyond that, my books are mysteries, and in keeping with the genre, I feel that by the end of a mystery some type of progression should have taken place, whether it's the revelation of the killer or an understanding of means and motives.

So, having said that, here are the beginning sentences from both the prologues AND the epilogues in my Tory Travers/David Alvarez series:

Engineered for Murder:

> **Prologue: It was a cool, dry, clear night, characteristic of summer in El Paso. The night brought only temporary relief from the summer heat, when not even the barest hint of clouds sheltered the parched earth from the sun, shining relentlessly down on this far western part of Texas. The most recent memory of rain might be two, or even three weeks past. People died on nights like this.**

Epilogue: The journalism student and his girlfriend came to the Mesilla graveyard in the late afternoon, partially to avoid the relentless daytime heat, and partially because he wanted to photograph the way the late afternoon sunlight illuminated the dilapidated gravestones.

Framework for Death:

Prologue: It took Alicia Boyce a minute to realize that she was actually awake, because she hadn't been aware of falling asleep. Waking and sleeping seemed the same lately, both filled with a sense of anxious waiting. She looked at her watch. She had dozed for less than an hour, and she didn't hear any sounds from the next room. With any luck, the baby would sleep on for a while.

Epilogue: Upon waking, it took Rodney Keipper a moment to realize where he was. He'd never traveled in northern New Mexico, so his kindly host had explained the night before that the Indian name for the town was pronounced Chee-my-o.

Affirmative Reaction:

Prologue: She figured it came down to a choice between going to work or committing murder.

Epilogue: It was late in the afternoon, the last Friday in January, and Tory really should be on her way home, not taking one last look at a prospective job. But she was nervous, and work, as always, was a good distraction.

In the first book, I wanted to emphasize the importance of relentless heat in relationship to the violence that would follow. In the second book, I wanted to explore the consequences of becoming a fugitive. In the third book, my protagonist's devotion to her job once again involves her in murder and the present effect of past relationships.

It is interesting to look at these opening sentences as a progression of time passing while writing a series--it appears to me that my opening sentences are progressing toward that one-line-attention-grabber goal. Hopefully this means that one learns and grows as a writer, although it will be interesting to see how opening sentences vary as I explore other series. Perhaps I'll lose the need for balance and simply start out with "If you dare peek at the last page of this book for an easy answer while I've suffered and sweated to disguise the identity of the killer, you'll discover that the whole thing is rigged to blow up in your face!"

Now, how's THAT for an opening sentence?

***

"Well, places to go, people to kill, and all that..." Janne Kafka Skipper

---

Mary Jo Putney
http://www.maryjoputney.com

Opening is an interesting subject for a book. As you probably know, it's an old writer's saying that the first few pages sell a book, and the last few pages sell your next book.

On the whole, I can't say that I'm particularly great at dynamite openings. Generally I open slowly, setting the scene. One of the most memorable first lines I've done was for *Shattered Rainbows*:

She needed a husband, and she needed one fast.

Another good one was for *Silk and Shadows*:

He called himself Peregrine, the wanderer, and he came to London for revenge.

What a good opening needs is to intrigue the reader enough to continue. Most often this is done by raising questions, such as "Why on earth does this woman need a husband so fast?" More broadly, "Who are these people, and why are they doing this?" Sometimes writers are urged to start with fast action, but for me, action isn't very interesting if I don't know or care about the people involved, so pure action won't usually grab me. Interesting people and/or settings will.

Very often, I start a book with a prologue that shows one of the protagonists at a psychologically significant moment, such as a little girl scrounging to survive along the docks, or a man thinking about how the whole of his dangerous, dramatic life has been in preparation for this moment. A snapshot in the "real time" of a prologue can define that character more vividly than pages of flashback later in the story.

Off the Shelf

He didn't want to be there.
Nora Roberts, *Hidden Riches*, 1994

For more than two hundred years, the Owens women have been blamed for everything that has gone wrong in town.
Alice Hoffman, *Practical Magic*, 1995

I sat on my living room sofa at five o'clock in the morning with a copy of the mock-up of the front page of the day's *New York Post* in my hand, looking at my own obituary.
Linda Fairstein, *Final Jeopardy*, 1996

The air was raw with February the morning Bobby Lee Fuller found the first body.
Nora Roberts, *Carnal Innocence*, 1991

Jail is not as bad as you might imagine.
Anna Quindlen, *One True Thing*, 1994

Snow fell in the woods, drifted deep, a pristine starlit world in which a single winter hare made significance--slow advance from a wandering footprinted time past into a white unwritten time to come.
C.J. Cherryh, *Chernevog*, 1990

Chuck woke in a sweat, his heart pounding as hard as it had twenty-odd years before.
Stuart Woods, *Choke*, 1995

"Funerals work best in the rain," said Robert Natchez.
Laurence Shames, *Scavenger Reef*, 1994

Tall, red-haired Abigail MacQueen leapt from slick boulder to boulder above the swirl and shift of foaming green water.
Karen Harper, *The Wings of Morning*, 1993

Bryan DeCourcey Cavanaugh had a chameleon reputation.
Morris West, *The Lovers*, 1993

"Promise me, Kate, that you won't let this ruin Christmas."
Elizabeth Forsythe, *Hailey Home Free*, 1991

The summer my father bought the bear, none of us was born--we were even conceived: not Frank, the oldest; not Frannie, the loudest; not me, the next; and not the youngest of us Lilly and Egg.
John Irving, *The Hotel New Hampshire*, 1981

Jack Torrance thought: Officious little prick.
Stephen King, *The Stand*, 1977

Awakened with a sudden start, as though someone had touched my shoulder, and I half expected to see Andrew standing over me as I blinked in the dim room.
Barbara Taylor Bradford, *Everything to Gain*, 1994

There was a wall.
Ursula Leguin, *The Dispossessed,* 1974

"I've watched through his eyes, I've listened through his ears, and I tell you he's the one. Or at least as close as we're going to get."
Orson Scott Card, *Ender's Game*, 1977

The secret service holds much that is kept secret even from very senior officers in the organization.
Ian Fleming, *The Man with the Golden Gun*, 1965

The first time I saw Brenda, she asked me to hold her glasses.
Philip Roth, *Goodbye Columbus*, 1959

On the morning of August 8, 1965, Robert Kincaid locked the door to his small two-room apartment on the third floor of a rambling house in Bellingham, Washington.
Robert Waller, *Bridges of Madison County*, 1992

Insomnia?
Claudia Crawford, *Bliss*, 1994

It was a filthy place to raise kids.
Terrell L. Bowers, *Tanner's Last Chance*, 1991

On December 22, 1958, only two days before, they had been safe in London.
Richard Condon, *Mile High*, 1969

Eileen Putman
http://www.eileenputman.com

Most readers want to plunge right into a story, not wade through a prologue. They dislike prologues for the same reason authors find them convenient: a prologue presents background or precipitating events that might disrupt narrative flow if included later in the story. It's a nifty device for avoiding the flashbacks and lengthy explanations that can bog a novel down.

Because readers must accept the inconvenience of a prologue, their standards are exacting: The unwritten contract between readers and authors demands that a prologue be short and compelling. It must open and end with a bang, moving inexorably toward Chapter One while persuading the reader that the prologue was time well spent.

Here's the opening of my prologue for *Never Trust a Rake*, an Avon historical romance:

> **He wasn't about to traipse all over England looking for virgins. Not as long as Our Lady of Mercy convent lay cheek to jowl with the Market Street dock, where his new boat bobbed in waters swollen by high tide. With any luck, he could be on his way before the tide went out.**
>
> **Like most of the ladies he met, luck danced to his tune. This very night, luck had dealt him a royal flush and the Earl of Sedbury a measly pair of tens, thereby gifting him with the earl's trim little yacht. Luck had not given**

him the courage to sneak into a convent full of sleeping nuns, but he had found that in the earl's wine.

My editor thought the first line was a great "hook;" I'm not exactly sure why. Perhaps it has to do with the conventions of romances set in England's Regency period, when a peer's duty was to marry a chaste girl and immediately impregnate her to secure the "purity" of the family line. In Regency romance, British lords and virgins belong together, rather like bees and flowers.

With this historical, I wanted to turn those conventions around. The opening line was a wry promise to readers that this jaded hero's road to romantic happiness would be a bit different. Sure enough, he quickly tangles with a chamber-pot wielding Mother Superior. That sets up Chapter One, where he ends up on the wrong end of a noose and is rescued by the most inveterate virgin he's ever had the misfortune to meet: the heroine.

It's only now, deconstructing this opening, that I've given any thought to why it works. To be sure, it's meant to draw the reader into the hero's world and the disaster precipitated by his reckless prank. Yet we also sympathize with him and his ironic world view, for what self-respecting hero has not found himself in the middle of the night railing against the conventions that force him to be something he is not?

As we sometimes rail against ourselves, and perhaps that's the real secret: contemporary or historical, the story must resonate with the reader. The moment that happens, you have your "hook"--wry, or otherwise.

Charles Wilson
http://usr.metamall.com/~cwilson/index.html

For a new author trying to gain a following, not only is the first sentence the most important sentence in a book, the first paragraph is the most important paragraph, the first page is the most important page, and the first chapter is the most important chapter.

There is a very simple reason why this is true: If the book jacket and cover copy of a book interests a reader who has never heard of the author, the reader is usually going to open the first page or so and read to see if they like A) the story's start, and B) the way the writer puts his words down on paper.

This is your chance to throw in words that "attract," and do it in a way that "sounds like" you can write.

The sentence (or paragraph) doesn't have to be complicated; it only has to have something that attracts. For example, in my first mystery/psychological thriller, *Nightwatcher*--a book intended to be scary or tension-filled--I used a very simple line to attract readers looking for this type of story:

> **It was an unsettled night at the John H. Douglas Hospital for the Insane, the smell of an impending storm in the air.**

When the line is dissected, you see the reader is immediately hit with NIGHT, with INSANE, with IMPENDING STORM--All things that, by word association, start off as being something scary or tension building. The rest of the opening paragraph builds on that, with a lone, young nurse crossing between patient dormitories at the complex.

You can vary this approach. For example, prologues are best used to tell enough of the story--by setting the scene--to attract the reader into the remainder of the story. They are often used when something has happened in the past, and the story itself is going to start several years, decades, whatever, later.

For example, in my novel, *Game Plan*, a story of a military experiment gone bad, I use a prologue to show five criminals, experimental volunteers whose minds have been greatly enhanced by computer chips implanted in their brains, escaping from the military facility where the chips have been implanted. This sets up the actual story, which starts in Chapter One--ten years later.

It is important here to use words that create TENSION, or words that quickly peak the reader's interest. The prologue starts:

She came silently down the wide corridor, moving swiftly, but not running. The only things that took away from her youthful beauty were two tiny blemishes spaced a few inches apart on her forehead, and the United States Disciplinary Barracks garb she wore— shapeless trousers and shirt in faded blue colors. Six months since she had been brought to this place and they still made her wear the hated garments. Six months and she could still visualize the razor wire of Leavenworth, still smell the concrete walls....

In the start of that paragraph you have someone "MOVING SWIFTLY." It is a young, beautiful woman--what is she doing? She was a convict from Leavenworth. Why is she there? All of the words add to the tension and make the reader WONDER?

EXCITE THE READER.

MAKE the reader want to read more.

---

10 -- Full Circle

As we said in chapter one, the first sentence begins the relationship between reader and author. The story's end is a promise fulfilled. This last chapter wraps up with the authors who chose to write about a book's circular theme and endings as they relate to beginnings.

After an intriguing, suspenseful story, the end resolves the conflicts, solves any mysteries, and implies the theme of the entire story. Obviously, authors often spend as much time on the ending as they do the opening to achieve this full circle ending.

When the end echoes the opening, it provides a powerful closure.

The reader will be anticipating that author's next book!

Insights

Lee Harris
http://www.NMOMysteries.com   (Nuns, Mothers and Others, what the writing team of Lee Harris, Jonnie Jacobs, Lora Roberts, and Valerie Wolzien calls themselves)

In my first mystery, *The Good Friday Murder*, I knew when I wrote the first sentence that the sense of it would also be the last sentence in the book.   I'm one of those people that enjoys completing circles. In this book my sleuth, Christine Bennett, a young woman who was released from her vows as a Franciscan nun only three weeks earlier, is getting used to the secular life inch by inch, as it were. But old habits die hard and one of those she has little control over is the cycle of waking and sleeping. The first sentence is:

I still get up at five in the morning.

Little by little the reader learns of the kind of schedule Chris adhered to in her life in the convent, rising early, saying prayers, eating breakfast, performing charges (chores) at the convent, and so on. By evening, the nuns are tired early and retire early.

The book takes Chris through the first month or so of her new life. She learns how to select clothes, have a real haircut, put meals together, even go out with a man on a date. But when all is said and done, after she solves a forty-year-old murder and gets to know her way around Brooklyn and meets a neighbor who becomes a friend, nature has its way. She gives a party on a weekend afternoon, cleans up after her guests and falls into bed early.

I still wake up at five o'clock in the morning.

Laura Lynn Leffers
http://www.sff.net/people/laura-lynn-leffers

"Hey babe!"

starts off my first novel, *Dance on the Water*, as the protagonist, Belle MacKay, is verbally accosted by a group of hormonally inept boys. Their taunts touch off transition for Belle who, as she confronts her hecklers (and scares the zits off their noses, doing it), is consequently thrust into a confrontation with her own reality: a life filled with avoidance.

Once Belle begins to face her reality everything changes, and it signals the theme of a story in which all of the comfortable "walls" she's built to make her life bearable begin to topple. Her battles change as her convenient lifestyle dissolves, as she moves through starting over in a far more primitive place, in a cottage on a tiny island in a northern Indiana lake. Building to the biggest battle of her life, one in which she desperately needs the ability to discern reality, her struggle pays dividends when the long-dead native American ancestors she seeks return to give her the greatest gift she will ever need: love, and the strength of family.

That spiritual reality empowers her life because she's no longer a victim. The end of the book comes full circle to its beginning, in which Belle took charge of her own reality and began her transition.

My second novel, *Out of the Blue*, deals with abandonment. Its female protagonist has never allowed herself to be victimized by being abandoned, pregnant; instead, she's gone on with her life, has raised her daughter to young womanhood, has made for herself a full life despite, it seems, some bad choices.

This book begins with its male protagonist, who has made no life for himself at all. I chose to begin the story with this character, Carey Callahan, because it's his action that begins the story, and because it was his inaction that caused the first of the abandonment issues the book deals with. *Blue*'s opening scene, then, shows Carey looking at his hands:

There were lines in his skin he'd never noticed.

His hands, shaking, are holding a letter received twenty years too late, which tells him he has a child.

Carey begins a journey that causes many levels of abandonment issues (including his own) to be confronted and, eventually, resolved. Hands which, in the beginning of the book, are shown as ineffectual and untrustworthy have become constructive and caring by the end of the book. Carey's journey is the catalyst for the female protagonist's transition, and for forcing other issues-- including a deadly, greed-based motivation--rather like the Mousetrap game in which the ball, having begun its course, is unstoppable until it forces that poor jerk to dive into the washtub.

My next book, currently titled *Portrait of Bright*, is about injustices and their consequences: An act of rape in the past colors everything with a glaze the book's protagonist, an oil painter named

Claire, can't see through. The story begins, therefore, with a painting in progress, one that depicts far more than Claire, its creator, realizes. Its opening line is:

> **It was all in the painting. All of it, the pieced-together, patched-up and stuck-closed-with-chewing-gum kind of existence these folks lived, if only I'd thought to look.**

When Claire chooses to accept a commission, contracting to paint a portrait of an unlovely one year-old, she's worried about normal things like perspectives, likenesses, and the behavior of a child. She doesn't realize she needs worry more about perspective perceptions, the true look of a madwoman; she learns to concern herself more with the behavior of the adults in her line of vision, than that of the child. She doesn't know that this choice, taken to begin a professional career, could well be her last.

Each of our seemingly small choices in life are potential beginnings. I love imagining where those beginnings could lead.

Happy reading, inspired writing.

Dean Ing

The opening words of *Flying to Pieces* are:

> **If Elmo Benteen hadn't raised so much hell at his last BOF party, he might've lived to throw another one. Or maybe not; Elmo was loopy as a bedspring, having fought off half the tropical diseases known to medical science and too much of the VD.**

I opened *Wild Country*, a science fiction western, with the terse, blunt,

> **Death minus three minutes and counting.**

And the very first passage of *The Skins of Dead Men*, a thriller about a tough little schoolteacher, drops her into slam-bang action with,

> **So what was T. C. supposed to do, armed with a tire iron and confronted by the two guys hauling a terrified seven-year-old off like a sack of meal? Once she got a glimpse of the boy, the rest was pure adrenaline, and pure T. C.**

It's obvious I wanted these stories to hit running. But *Flying* was comedic, with a bunch of tacky, geriatric hardnoses. The opener, I trust, hinted at that. There's something paramilitary about "...three minutes and counting," and, coupled with the title *Wild Country*, I'm implying heavy action -- SOON -- and that military buffs might enjoy it. My heroine T. C. takes a role usually reserved for males; to make her convincing I'd best present her that way up front. And why would a glance at the boy make her so steroidal? Readers are invited to be curious. T.C. is well-intentioned but naive. That opening passage reflects her uncomplicated ways.

In other books I open with a more measured pace, as in *The Ransom of Black Stealth One*, which I won't quote here. It starts more slowly, darkly, as my favorite spy stories do. Maybe that's a mistake, but it sold a third of a million copies so it worked. But it didn't have a powerful hook up front. What it had was my usual implied contract with readers.

Because I write different kinds of books, I give readers a fair notion of what to expect from the opener. That's my promise, and I try hard to keep it; I want readers to know I'm dependable. It shouldn't be surprising that my openings lines are sometimes the ones I polish last of all.

Off the Shelf

Troubled faces had begun to look alike to me.
Jonathan Valin, *Day of Wrath*, 1982

And now Cynthia was on about her son again; her confounded dream son.
Michael Innes, *Carson's Conspiracy*, 1984

Jolie was in France when she felt the pain.
Piers Anthony, *And Eternity*, 1990

Samuel Wilders's teeth grated together with each bump and jolt of the wagon.
Gary D. Svee, *Single Tree*, 1994

"Most train robbers ain't smart, which is a lucky thing for the railroads," Call said.
Larry McMurtry, *Streets of Laredo*, 1993

Dusk settled down about the Fourlands, a slow graying of light, a gradual lengthening of shadows.
Terry Brooks, *The Talismans of Shannara*, 1993

The tropical rain fell in drenching sheets, hammering the corrugated roof of the clinic building, roaring down the metal gutters, splashing on the ground in a torrent.
Michael Crichton, *Jurassic Park*, 1990

When stealth means survival, man can outdo a coyote.
Wesley Ellis, *Lone Star and the Timberland Terror*, 1986

On December 8th, 1915, Meggie Cleary had her fourth birthday.
Colleen McCullough, *The Thorn Birds*, 1982

The large ballroom was crowded with familiar ghosts come to help celebrate her birthday.
Sidney Sheldon, *Master of the Game*, 1982

If I am out of my mind, it's all right with me, thought Moses Herzog.
Saul Bellow, *Herzog*, 1961

The door swung shut silently behind them, cutting off the light, music, and wild celebration of the ballroom.
Joan D. Vinge, *The Snow Queen*, 1980

I hope it will not be too much of a shock to you to get a letter from your son-in-law.
Willard Temple, *The Drip Dried Tourist*, 1969

It is not given to many of us to pinpoint the actual moment of our entry into a world of new beginnings.
R.F. Delderfield, *Mr. Sermon*, 1963

In the Arkansas Ozarks the times weren't easy that war summer of 1861.
Will Henry, *One More River to Cross*, 1967

"That woman called today."
Helen Van Slyke, *No Love Lost*, 1980

The gun was jarringly out of place.
Jacqueline Briskin, *Everything and More*, 1983

The first thing that I noticed that Saturday night was the group of teenagers dressed in black leaning against the wall of the bank, four guys in jeans and leather jackets watching the street too attentively.
Linda Grant, *Vampire Bytes*, 1998

The rain was falling in a sweet relentless fashion as it does in spring in London and it was all very peaceful and pleasant, if uncompromisingly wet.
Margery Allingham, *Cargo of Eagles*, 1968

It seemed as I tossed and turned far into the night, maddened by a dripping tap I was too irresolute to fix, that I owed too many people too many things.
Christopher Hodder-Williams, *The Egg-Shaped Thing*, 1967

"I've got to get out," Hal Yarrow could hear someone muttering from a great distance.
Philip Jose Farmer, *The Lovers*, 1961

The month before her wedding to the third richest man in the second largest city in Ohio, Lily Blair awoke in the middle of the night and realized that she did not want to get married.
Janice Harayda, *The Accidental Bride*, 1999

Going to see Clare's family on the isolated hilltop where Ralph Quick had built his domestic fortress was an ordeal for Julia.
Gail Godwin, *A Southern Family*, 1987

The word sounded alien in his mouth, as if spoken by someone else.
Michael Connelly, *Angels Flight*, 1999

"Damn it, this isn't about opening another hotel, JL, it's about your obsession with revenge."
Jayne Ann Krentz, *Eye of the Beholder*, 1999

Olivia was four when the monster came.
Nora Roberts, *River's End*, 1999

Not every king would care to start his reign with the wholesale massacre of children.
Mary Stewart, *The Last Enchantment*, 1979

Sleep eluded her.
Barbara Taylor Bradford, *Remember*, 1991

Take My Wife, Please... ©
Tara K. Harper
http://www.teleport.com/~until/tkh.htm

Many writers treat the first line of a book primarily as a hook for the reader--it is just a way to get people curious enough to continue into the story. To me, it is more than that: it is the first step in a new direction and a forecasting of what is to come. Every phrase that follows should spring from the first line because those initial words are an introduction to new thoughts, startling questions, unusual ideas, and the expansion of your own world into new realms.

Although a writer might strive for an opening line that is shocking, moody, intriguing, or moving, he does not, in general, want a sentence--or book--that is gimmicky or contrived. For example, formula novels always seem to contain an obligatory sex-drugs-violence-depravity scene in the first chapter in order to provide a generic assurance that there will be action in the story. In the same vein, many modern novelists seem to be writing formula first lines as if these hook-the-reader phrases are the final words of a story--like punch lines misplaced at the beginnings of books.

The more I read, the more I appreciate a less contrived, more openly structured first sentence--a line that is not an obvious slap in the face, but which tells me there might be something of substance in the novel. One that suggests an interesting image, poses an unexpected question, or which indicates that the writer has skill enough to unfold the ideas and develop the story, not simply rely on an easy one-liner to bring me into the book.

A book's plotline is simple--it's just a string of facts and dates, names and events. It is what it is, and there's really not much excitement to it. But a story, like life, is not just a set of events. It is poetry and balance, dance and desire, violence and horror and fear. It is startlement and epiphany and a growth from one moment into the next. The first line of a book should be an introduction to that intrigue, not an end unto itself.

Personally, I prefer using short, direct first lines because every profound or intriguing experience and change in my life has begun with a single movement. It isn't usually a shocking or unusual step that starts an adventure; it is a simple inquiry—such as, what does human DNA really look like? Or, how deep can I skin dive? What is it like to wrestle a cougar? Can I face the stillness? Life shoots off in curious directions and offers astounding discoveries from such straightforward questions. And so, each moment in life--and in a story--is like an unlimited movement forward--or backward, depending on how terrifying or horrible the moment is--like walking on sharks while body surfing, or helping someone die.

As a writer, I have found that my first lines reflect my attitude toward life. They are usually short statements that have no great or fancy meaning in themselves, but are simply pointers to the events that follow; just as, in life, each moment is meaningless by itself because, like a bare truth, it has no context. But woven together, the moments become patterns with color and complexity, and therein lies the heart of every book. A first line should not be a story's most memorable element; it should be an introduction to the ideas and the wealth of words that follow.

Some Favorite Opening Lines ...

> **Chronic remorse, as all the moralists are agreed, is a most undesirable sentiment.** From the foreword of Aldous Huxley's *Brave New World*

> **Granted: I am an inmate of a mental hospital; my Keeper is watching me, he never lets me out of his**

sight; there's a peephole in the door, and my keeper's eye is the shade of brown that can never see through a blue-eyed type like me. *The Tin Drum,* Gunter Grass

First of all, it was October, a rare month for boys.
Something Wicked this Way Comes, Ray Bradbury

When shall we three meet again
In thunder, lightning, or in rain?
Macbeth, William Shakespeare.

Although I've always liked this line by itself, the emotional response it evokes from me is actually from what comes after it, not from those words themselves. It is that response that makes the sentence one of the most powerful first lines I've ever read. After the play, that opening question comes back as a reminder of everything that followed—everything that I, Macbeth, Malcolm, Lady Macbeth, and the others have been through. This truly is the perfect first line, because it reasserts itself after the play with all the depth and conflict and humanity of the story, not just its own few words.

Yvonne Navarro
http://www.para-net.com/~ynavarro

I thought this was going to be easy.

Until I realized that all four of the solo novels I've had published so far all start quite differently. If I look at my short stories, it's easy to see the pattern of starting right in the middle of dramatic dialogue, catching the reader's interest by throwing them in the midst of everything right *now.* But novels are a different creature altogether, and they can run in either direction-- in one, a single, electric sentence might be just the trick, while in another you need a carefully sculpted page to build up to that oh-so-perfect moment.

In three of these four novels (*AfterAge, Final Impact,* and *Red Shadows*), I've more or less destroyed mankind, and in one (*deadrush*) the potential was always there if the... "problem" wasn't halted. Stepping back and studying these four openings, I think what a reader is unconsciously looking to get in those first few paragraphs is a question that he or she *must* have answered.

Why so I think that? Well, take a look:

In *AfterAge*, the point of no return comes at the end of a very short, half-page prologue, with the simple statement:

> **But those who inherited the earth were not meek at all.**
> (*Who-- or what-- inherited the earth?*)

In *Deadrush*, the very first sentence does it:

> **"God help us," the old woman whispered.** *(What's wrong?!)*

Final Impact starts much more softly, a short paragraph following the thoughts of an American Indian child as she asks her own unanswerable question:

> **My skin is red. What is... red?** (*Why doesn't she know what 'red' is?*)

And finally, in *Red Shadows*, the simple declaration by Scanlon O'Rysley at the start of Chapter One,

> **He felt like God.**

raises a flurry of them. (*Who is he, and why/how could he feel like God? What's he done or is doing now to feel this way?*)

So the goal is not just to open a book, but to form an unspoken question-- which then leads to another, and another, and another-- all of which instill in your reader a curiosity that can only be satisfied at the end of several hundred pages by the words "The End."

Off the Shelf

He had played this same game before and had anticipated this time it would be something of a letdown.
Mary Higgins Clark, *You Belong to Me*, 1998

Two years into his sixties, Duane Moore—a man who had driven pickups for as long as he had been licensed to drive—parked his pickup in his own carport one day and began to walk wherever he went.
Larry McMurtry, *Duane's Depressed*, 1999

The dove-colored Chevrolet was parked fifty feet from the hospital entrance.
Ellery Queen, *Inspector Queen's Own Case*, 1956

Carmichael might have been the only person west of the Rocky Mountains that morning who didn't know what was going on.
Robert Silverberg, *The Alien Years*, 1998

"Mr. Leopold Gantvoort is not at home," the servant who opened the door said, "but his son, Mr. Charles is—if you wish to see him."
Dashiell Hammett, *The Continental Op*, 1923

At first Gill assumed it was just another bit of space debris, winking as it turned around its own axis and sending bright flashes of reflected light down where they were placing the cable around AS-64-B1.3.
Anne McCaffrey and Margaret Ball, *Acorna: The Unicorn Girl*, 1997

"There is a dead horse lying in the street," she said.
Vina Delmar, *The Big Family*, 1961

The San Francisco's Tenderloin is a twenty-square block district that contains some of the greatest contrasts in the city.
Marcia Muller, *There's Nothing to Be Afraid Of*, 1985

If I had dreamed that what I was doing would get me involved with the Sacramento Police Department, particularly with Captain Rose and Sgt. Huber, I wouldn't have been walking south on Third Street that sunny May morning.
Don Blunt, *Dead Giveaway*, 1963

The heart of London is large; to some it is warm, to other, perhaps to very many others, it is as cold as ice.
John Creasey, *A Bundle for the Toff*, 1967

Sometimes Hugh Brenner thought he'd been born on the wrong planet.
James P. Hogan, *Paths to Otherwhere*, 1996

Nick Naylor had been called many things since becoming chief spokesman for the Academy of Tobacco Studies, but, until now, no one had actually compared him to Satan.
Christopher Buckley, *Thank You for Smoking*, 1994

Robert E. Lee paused to dip his pen once more in the inkwell.
Harry Turtledove, *The Guns of the South*, 1992

Martha Ingram had come to Rome to escape something; George Hartwell had been certain of it from the first.
Elizabeth Spencer, *Knights and Dragons*, 1965

Chase Dalton emptied the bottle and scowled at the half-filled glass.
Giles A. Lutz, *The Turnaround*, 1978

Gone Tomorrow was a community that had been born only days ago, and soon it would be no more.
Cliff Farrell, *Owl Hoot Trail*, 1971

In the spring of 1971, when it became apparent to Howard W. Amberson that neither he nor his wife had much time remaining, he walked to Woolworth's and purchased a large ledger, bound in red and gray.
Don Robertson, *Praise the Human Season*, 1974

The planning of her wardrobe and the subject of clothes had never, for Valle Montgomery, occupied more than a tiny, unregarded corner of her mind.
Joan Aiken, *Castle Barebane*, 1976

Once my mother phoned me and said, "Oh, why did the mother in your story have to be so slangy?"
Jessamyn West, *The Life I Really Lived*, 1979

"When you finally set yourself alight," Maeve Starzynski said, **"don't come crying to me."**
Bob Shaw, *Fire Pattern*, 1984

I met Jack Kennedy in November, 1946.
Norman Mailer, *An American Dream*, 1964

I get the willies when I see closed doors.
Joseph Heller, *Something Happened*, 1966

The temperature hit ninety degrees the day she arrived.
Jacqueline Susann, *Valley of the Dolls*, 1966

Not to every young girl is it given to enter the harem of the Sultan of Turkey and return to her homeland a virgin.
Dorothy Dunnett, *The Ringed Castle*, 1971

When I finally caught up with Abraham Trahearne, he was drinking beer with an alcoholic bulldog named Fireball Roberts in a ramshackle joint just outside of Sonoma, California, drinking the heart right out of a fine spring afternoon.
James Crumley, *The Last Good Kiss*, 1978

Romance Authors' Pseudonyms

Some of these romance authors write under more than one pseudonym.

Pseudonym	Author Name
Victoria Holt	Eleanor Burford Hibbert
Elizabeth Peters	Barbara Mertz
Barbara Michaels	Barbara Mertz
Ursula Torday	Paula Allardyce
Philippa Carr	Eleanor Burford Hibbert
Jude Deveraux	Jude Gilliam White
Valerie Sherwood	Jeanne Hines
Jean Plaidy	Eleanor Burford Hibbert

Mystery & Western Authors' Pseudonyms

Some of these authors write under more than one pseudonym.

Pseudonym	Author Name
Anthony Morton	John Creasey
Evan Hunter	Salvatore Lombino
Fritz Leiber	Francis Lathrop
David Axton	Dean R. Koontz
K.R. Dwyer	Dean R. Koontz
John Loxmith	John Brunner
Matilda Hughes	Charlotte Macleod
Robert Caine Frazer	John Creasey
Tex Burns	Louis L'Amour
Dr. A	Isaac Asimov
Kyle Hunt	John Creasey
Paul French	Isaac Asimov
Richard Marsten	Salvatore Lombino
Ed McBain	Salvatore Lombino
James Marsden	John Creasey
Brian Coffey	Dean R. Koontz
Trevor Staines	John Brunner
Hunt Collins	Salvatore Lombino
Keith Woodcott	John Brunner
Ezra Hannon	Salvatore Lombino
J.J. Marric	John Creasey
Alisa Craig	Charlotte Macleod
Philip Latham	Robert S. Richardson
Jack Foxx	Bill Pronzini
Alex Saxon	Bill Pronzini

Ellen Kushner
http://www.wgbh.org/pri/spirit

To me, the rhythm of an opening sentence is more important than the information it contains. Language, after all, is music on the page; it's not just the eye and the brain you want to appeal to, but the ear. As Duke Ellington said, "It don't mean a thing if it ain't got that swing!" The opening to my 1987 novel,

Swordspoint, is almost in two parts.   It leads with a simple, declarative statement,

Snow was falling on Riverside.

but then continues to pull you in with almost languid and very sensual language,

great white feather-puffs that veiled the cracks in the facades of its ruined houses, slowly softening the harsh contours of jagged roof and fallen beam.

(Try reading it aloud and you'll see what I mean!)

The lovely thing about writing is that it can appeal to many senses at once: I'm also trying to set up a picture in your mind, like a long shot introducing a little town in a movie. (Odd, because I'm not a movie fan - but I tend to write rather cinematically! Maybe because my first love was theatre.)   Of course, the joke of the book's opening is that it's about deception: After carefully setting up this description of a fairy-tale town, I blow it up on the next page by saying that nothing you're imagining from the picture-perfect little scene, a standard opening for fantasy novels, is in fact true. I'm being honest with you right from the start about what to expect as you read this book--that what looks like a typical fantasy novel is not; that people may appear to be Good or Bad Guys and surprise you; that expectations will constantly be set up and blown up.

The ending of *Swordspoint* mirrors the beginning: After pages of intrigue, drama and high emotion, we are once again back above the city (up among the stars) in our role as watchers. The book opened on a winter's morning, and closes on a warm spring night, as life itself proceeds in its unpredictable infinite patterns - so unlike the measured dance of stars - until, for the satisfaction of their entertainment, the watchers choose a point at which to stop.

J. A. Lawrence

Once upon a time --now there's a catchy one -- my late husband, James Blish, explained how to start a story. Once upon a time, he said, there was a man who had a pet donkey. He loved the donkey beyond his life. Here cherished it, petted it, fed it the best straw and oats and carrots, called the vet if it sneezed -- the works. Neighbors thought him mad. One day he was called away from home. He sought far and wide for a donkey sitter and everyone told him of the man up the mountain, a sort of hermit, who was known to be wonderful with animals. Reluctant to leave his darling in anyone's charge, the man made his way slowly up the long hill, explaining tenderly to his pet that it would be all right, he would be back as fast as he could, and not to worry, everybody recommended this inspired caretaker.

He finally was persuaded to put the halter rope into the hands of the holy man, and cut short his tearful, fond farewells. As he plodded sadly down the mountain, he could not help but look back. Appalled, he caught the care-er in the act of bringing a stout 2-by-4 down on the head of the poor donkey. He rushed up and in horrified surprise gasped, "What do you think you are doing?"

"Don't worry," said the hermit soothingly. "You know, first you have to get their attention."

We used to play a game --Rewriting Famous Opening Sentences. Would "Call me George" have the same impact as "Call me Ishmael?" "I shall never return to -- Boston"? "Once upon a time there was a Martian named Wolfgang Amadeus Mozart." (Actually, that's not bad.)

So when I was musing over my first serious story, the first sentence came to me:

I hate it when my eyes bleed.

Oho! So who says this? Why? I had been considering the implications of the Inquisitor's question in "The Brothers Karamazov," which led me to think of an induced illness for a good cause. That theme disappeared as I studied auto-immune diseases, and long before the real Boy in the Bubble was known or AIDS was discovered, I had worked out a character in just that position --whose eyes would bleed every now and then. The story was called "Opening Problem," after the first move in a chess game.

I love intriguing openers, though I don't always find them -- and also snappy last sentences, the kind that act as a flick of the tale as the story goes off stage.

Off the Shelf

When he was sleepless, which was less often than it used to be, Jess Stone would get into the black Explorer he'd driven from L.A. and cruise around Paradise, Massachusetts, where he was chief of police.
Robert B. Parker, *Trouble in Paradise*, 1998

Ziantha stood before the door smoothing a tight-fitting glove with her other hand.
Andre Norton, *Forerunner Foray*, 1973

It was in that year when the fashion in cruelty demanded not only the crucifixion of peasant children, but a similar fate for their pets, that I first met Lucifer and was transported into Hell; for the Prince of Darkness wished to strike a bargain with me.
Michael Moorcock, *The War Hound and the World's Pain*, 1981

Close your eyes.
Joe Haldeman, *All My Sins Remembered*, 1977

In the sunlight in the center of a ring of trees Lev sat cross-legged, his head bent above his hands.
Ursula Leguin, *The Eye of the Heron*, 1978

"Never take anything for granted. Fate or the devil has a way of kicking you up the backside when you least expect it," my grandfather used to say in his coarse way, not that it ever treated him so cavalierly and I never realized how right he was until one night in the summer of 1829.
Constance Heaven, *Lord of Ravensley*, 1978

Because he thought that he would have problems taking the child over the border into Canada, he drove south, skirting the cities whenever they came and taking the anonymous freeways which were like a separate country as travel was itself like a separate country.
Peter Straub, *Ghost Story*, 1979

It began the way that the end of the world will begin, with a telephone call that comes at three in the morning.
Ross Thomas, *If You Can't Be Good*, 1973

The cellar was divided into rooms.
Ruth Rendell, *A Demon in My View*, 1976

A man with binoculars.
Michael Crichton, *The Andromeda Strain*, 1969

"Have you seen the skeleton? I am sitting on it."
Jon Cleary, *The Fall of an Eagle*, 1964

Helen Ranston smiled sadly to herself, while she sat waiting for her husband to die.
Rog Phillips, *The Involuntary Immortals*, 1959

I am always drawn back to places where I have lived, the houses and their neighborhoods.
Truman Capote, *Breakfast at Tiffany's*, 1950

The younger living room would be a comfortable and well-ordered room if it were not for a number of indestructible contradictions to this state of being.
Lorraine Hansberry, *A Raisin in the Sun*, 1958

He rolled the cigarette in his lips, liking the taste of the tobacco, squinting his eyes against the sun glare.
Louis L'Amour, *Hondo*, 1953

May I, monsieur, offer my services without running the risk of intruding?
Albert Camus, *The Fall*, 1956

He knew he had let himself go.
William Shambaugh, *Cameron*, 1981

I limped into town.
Robin Gibson, *Ma Calhoun's Boys*, 1992

He found her in his bed.
Julie Garwood, *One Red Rose*, 1997

It was probably the cutest tush he had ever seen.
Sandra Brown, *Send No Flowers*, 1984

When we lived on Menard Avenue, I used to lie half-awake listening to my parents' conversation after the Bing Crosby program or Amos and Andy.
Andrew M. Greeley, *A Midwinter's Tale*, 1998

The stone was quartzite and the drill was dull—yet Harrigan sank the hole rapidly, swinging the twelve-pound hammer in a sort of fury.
Max Brand, *The Gauntlet*, 1998

"Help us, please."
The woman stood just inside the glass doors leading into the department. She cradled a little girl against her chest. The child's arms and legs hung limply toward the floor.
Charles Wilson, *Donor*, 1999

It was a great buffalo hunt that year one of the best in the memory of the People.
Don Coldsmith, *The Medicine Knife*, 1988

Tara had not worn white since her wedding day.
Wilber Smith, *Rage*, 1987

Right now, Clay Ballard was sorry he had picked up the middle-aged couple with their stalled covered wagon and delicate young blonde who had paid to ride out with them.
Bob Jasper, *Feud at Sundown*, 1951

Woman's lying in bed and the bed's on fire.
Don Winslow, *California Fire and Life*, 1999

Innocence is a bitch.
Carolyn Wheat, *Sworn to Defend*, 1998

She was seated at a table in the center of the prison yard, in a straight-backed chair, the legs of which were slightly uneven and wobbled uncertainly against the coarse and rocky soil.
Amy Ephron, *White Rose*, 1999

The body of Anderson Nez lay under a sheet on the gurney, waiting.
Tony Hillerman, *The First Eagle*, 1998

One day, Linc Marani vowed to himself he would drive a car like Kyle's and wear five-hundred-dollar suits.
James P. Hogan, *Outward Bound*, 1999

"The End" -- Promise Fulfilled

I asked the authors to join this project—to give original material on their views on opening sentences. They sure came through. Responding to this, each one provided his or her own slant. Some told what they perceived as their best openers and why they work; others have stories behind particular openers. Some authors shared a process to arrive at that special sentence; others revealed that they think opening sentences are not the kingpin, but only peripheral to the novel.

Some of them follow their example openers with what they were thinking when they penned them; how they work on those sentences; and ultimately the value they place on that first sentence.

Hooking the Reader spells out many ingredients for an attention-getting opener: Open with a bang, a whimper, an incongruous event, action, drama. Rhythm may be a part of it. Whether a long sentence is the hook, or a short, direct line, it has to pique the reader's interest. It's similar to giving a tasty bite—only a nibble—of the appetizer. Whoever reads that snappy, jarring, interesting opener will be compelled to relish the feast to come.

A few authors say that the opening doesn't matter to them: They treat every sentence with virtually the same care. They know that after the first paragraph, page, or chapter, their readers will be turning pages as fast as they can absorb the material printed.

Regardless, we have seen that the writer must be caught up in the story just as much as the reader will be.

One author, Frank Thompson, has fun with his work by always writing a passage that fits with the theme yet, unknown to us, conceals an inside joke. I thank Mr. Thompson for so candidly revealing this for the first time in *Hooking the Reader*.

Writers can take comfort from Carolyn Wheat, who says that the opening sentence is not as important as one may think. I found this to be true when I wrote my first fun book, instead of the usual technical manuals that paid the bills.

For the non-fiction *Living with Big Cats*, after the research, hours of interviews and transcription were finished, I evaluated what I had accumulated (approximately 400 pages). I knew which interviews and other parts went together, but I did not know how I would order the table of contents. In fact, a scene where a wild animal trainer has a close call could have gone to the chapter "Training Big Cats," or "Building a Relationship" (rapport between tiger and trainer).

For the previous fun books I wrote, I found the main thing in non-fiction is to write a chapter at a time. The chapters tell the writer where they best fit, just as in fiction the characters have the uncanny knack of taking over a plot.

The full circle, with a satisfying ending is personified by J. A. Lawrence who says that a satisfying book to her should be one with an intriguing opener and a snappy last sentence; the kind that acts as a flick of the tale as the story goes off stage.

Sharon Rendell-Smock
http://www.rendell-smock.com

Appendix A – Off the Classic Shelf

Yesterday, as today, a sincere wish to share a story, the skill to hook the reader, and oftentimes the need to put food on the table has been the common thread that binds successful authors into their unique guild of skilled artisans.

Imagine if you will Don Quixote without Cervantes' brilliant introduction to the hero and his way of life......difficult? You bet!

Try to enter the world of Mole and the riverbank friends, without Kenneth Grahame taking your hand to guide you through your shared adventures....you can't!

On the very first page of Wind in the Willows, Grahame plants in your mind the comforting thought that Spring has arrived, there's more to life than cleaning house, life itself is suddenly happier, less complicated and more secure.

Their skillful contributions are representative of the craft and enthusiasm needed to keep the reader hooked through and through, both in times past and now.

Two roads diverged in a yellow wood,
And sorry I could not travel both
And be one traveler, long I stood
And looked down one as far as I could
To where it bent in the undergrowth;
Then took the other, as just as fair,
And having perhaps the better claim,
Because it was grassy and wanted wear;
Though as for that the passing there
Had worn them really about the same,

And both that morning equally lay
In leaves no step had trodden black.
Oh, I kept the first for another day!
Yet knowing how way leads on to way,
I doubted if I should ever come back.

I shall be telling this with a sigh
Somewhere ages and ages hence:
Two roads diverged in a wood, and I—
I took the one less traveled by,
And that has made all the difference.
Robert Frost, *Mountain Interval*, 1920

Ours is essentially a tragic age, so we refuse to take it tragically.
D.H. Lawrence, *Lady Chatterley's Lover*, 1928

There was no hope for him this time: it was the third stroke.
James Joyce, *Dubliners*, 1916

All happy families are like one another; each unhappy family is
unhappy in its own way.
Leo Tolstoy, *Anna Karenina*, 1856

We were in class when the head-master came in, followed by a
"new fellow," not wearing the school uniform, and a school
servant carrying a large desk.
Gustave Flaubert, *Madame Bovary*, 1857

There was no possibility of taking a walk that day.
Charlotte Bronte, *Jane Eyre*, 1847

Mr. Sherlock Holmes, who was usually very late in the mornings, save upon those not infrequent occasions when he was up all night, was seated at the breakfast table.
Arthur Conan Doyle, *The Hound of the Baskervilles*, 1901

The towers of Zenith aspired above the morning mist; austere towers of steel and cement and limestone, sturdy as cliffs and delicate as silver rods. They were neither citadels nor churches, but frankly and beautifully office-buildings.
Sinclair Lewis, *Babbitt*, 1922

In a village of La Mancha, the name of which I have no desire to call to mind, there lived not long since one of those gentlemen that keep a lance in the lance-rack, an old buckler, a lean hack, and a greyhound for coursing.
Cervantes, *Don Quixote of La Mancha*, 1637

John T. Unger came from a family that had been well known in Hades--a small town on the Mississippi River--for several generations.
F. Scott Fitzgerald, *The Diamond as Big as the Ritz*, 1922

Half-way down a by-street of one of our New England towns, stands a rusty wooden house, with seven acutely peaked gables, facing towards various points of the compass, and a huge, clustered chimney in the midst.
Nathaniel Hawthorne, *The House of the Seven Gables*, 1851

The Mole had been working very hard all the morning, spring-cleaning his little home. First with brooms, then with dusters; then on ladders and steps and chairs, with a brush and a pail of whitewash; till he had dust in his throat and eyes, and splashes of whitewash all over his black fur, and an aching back and weary arms. Spring was moving in the air above and in the earth below and around him, penetrating even his dark and lowly little house with its spirit of divine discontent and longing. It was small wonder, then, that he suddenly flung down his brush on the floor, said `Bother!'
Kenneth Grahame, *Wind in the Willows*, 1908

The cold passed reluctantly from the earth, and the retiring fogs revealed an army stretched out on the hills, resting. As the landscape changed from brown to green, the army awakened, and began to tremble with eagerness at the noise of rumors.
Stephen Crane, *The Red Badge of Courage*, 1895

To go into solitude, a man needs to retire as much from his chamber as from society.
Ralph Waldo Emerson, *Nature*, 1836

You don't know about me without you have read a book by the name of The Adventures of Tom Sawyer; but that ain't no matter.
Mark Twain, *Huckleberry Finn*, 1884

The day broke gray and dull. The clouds hung heavily, and there was a rawness in the air that suggested snow. A woman servant came into a room in which a child was sleeping and drew the curtains. She glanced mechanically at the house opposite, a stucco house with a portico, and went to the child's bed.
W. Somerset Maugham, *Of Human Bondage*, 1915

A throng of bearded men, in sad-colored garments and gray, steeple-crowned hats, intermixed with women, some wearing hoods, and others bareheaded, was assembled in front of a wooden edifice, the door of which was heavily timbered with oak, and studded with iron spikes.
Nathaniel Hawthorne, *Scarlet Letter*, 1850

SQUIRE TRELAWNEY, Dr Livesey, and the rest of these gentlemen having asked me to write down the whole particulars about Treasure Island, from the beginning to the end, keeping nothing back but the bearings of the island, and that only because there is still treasure not yet lifted, I take up my pen in the year of grace 17 - , and go back to the time when my father kept the `Admiral Benbow' inn, and the brown old seaman, with the sabre cut, first took up his lodging under our roof.
Robert Louis Stevenson, *Treasure Island*, 1883

My father had a small Estate in Nottinghamshire; I was the Third of five Sons.
Jonathan Swift, *Gulliver's Travels*, 1726

I was born in the Year 1632, in the City of York, of a good Family, tho' not of that Country, my Father being a Foreigner of Bremen, who settled first at Hull: He got a good Estate by Merchandise, and leaving off his Trade, lived afterward at York, from whence he had married my Mother, Relations were named Robinson, a very good Family at Country, and from whom I was called Robinson Keutznaer; but by the usual Corruption of Words in England, we are now called, nay we call our Selves, and writer Name Crusoe, and so my Companions always call'd me.

Daniel De Foe, *The Life and Adventures of Robinson Crusoe*, 1716

It was the best of times, it was the worst of times, it was the age of wisdom, it was the age of foolishness, it was the epoch of belief, it was the epoch of incredulity, it was the season of Light, it was the season of Darkness, it was the spring of hope, it was the winter of despair, we had everything before us, we had nothing before us, we were all going direct to Heaven, we were all going direct the other way--in short, the period was so far like the present period, that some of its noisiest authorities insisted on its being received, for good or for evil, in the superlative degree of comparison only.

Charles Dickens, *A Tale of Two Cities*, 1859

Marley was dead: to begin with. There is no doubt whatever about that. The register of his burial was signed by the clergyman, the clerk, the undertaker, and the chief mourner. Scrooge signed it: and Scrooge's name was good upon `Change, for anything he chose to put his hand to. Old Marley was as dead as a door-nail.

Charles Dickens, *A Christmas Carol*, 1843

I am by birth a Genevese; and my family is one of the most distinguished of that republic.

Mary Shelley, *Frankenstein*, 1831

Alice was beginning to get very tired of sitting by her sister on the bank, and of having nothing to do: once or twice she had peeped into the book her sister was reading, but it had no pictures or conversations in it, "and what is the use of a book," thought Alice "without pictures or conversation?"

Lewis Carroll, *Alice's Adventures in Wonderland*, 1865

It must have been a little after three o'clock in the afternoon that it happened—the afternoon of June 3rd, 1916. It seems incredible that all that I have passed through--all those weird and terrifying experiences--should have been encompassed within so short a span as three brief months.
Edgar Rice Burroughs, *The Land That Time Forgot*, 1924

One thing was certain, that the white kitten had had nothing to do with it: -- it was the black kitten's fault entirely. For the white kitten had been having its face washed by the old cat for the last quarter of an hour (and bearing it pretty well, considering); so you see that it couldn't have had any hand in the mischief.
Lewis Carroll, *Through the Looking Glass*, 1872

It was a feature peculiar to the colonial wars of North America, that the toils and dangers of the wilderness were to be encountered before the adverse hosts could meet.
James Fenimore Cooper, *The Last of the Mohicans*, 1826

"TOM!"
No answer.
"TOM!"
No answer.
"What's gone with that boy, I wonder? You TOM!"
No answer.
Mark Twain, *The Adventures of Tom Sawyer*, 1876

How have I sinn'd, that this affliction Should light so heavy on me? I have no more sons, And this no more mine own.---My grand curse Hang o'er his head that thus transformed thee!---Travel? I'll send my horse to travel next. Monsieur Thomas.
Sir Walter Scott, *Rob Roy*, circa 1830

LOOK out! Look out, boys! Clear the track!
The witches are here! They've all come back!
They hanged them high,--No use! No use!
What cares a witch for a hangman's noose?
They buried them deep, but they wouldn't lie still,
For cats and witches are hard to kill;
They swore they shouldn't and wouldn't die,--
Books said they did, but they lie! they lie!
Oliver Wendell Holmes, *The Broomstick Train*, 1892

I was sick, sick unto death, with that long agony, and when they at length unbound me, and I was permitted to sit, I felt that my senses were leaving me.
Edgar Allan Poe, *The Pit and the Pendulum*, 1842

1801. - I have just returned from a visit to my landlord - the solitary neighbour that I shall be troubled with.
Emily Bronte, *Wuthering Heights*, 1864

The stranger came early in February one wintry day, through a biting wind and a driving snow, the last snowfall of the year, over the down, walking as it seemed from Bramblehurst railway station and carrying a little black portmanteau in his thickly gloved hand.
H. G. Wells, *The Invisible Man,* 1898

Jonathan Harker's Journal: 3 May. Bistritz. __Left Munich at 8:35 P. M, on 1st May, arriving at Vienna early next morning; should have arrived at 6:46, but train was an hour late. Buda-Pesth seems a wonderful place, from the glimpse which I got of it from the train and the little I could walk through the streets.
Bram Stoker, *Dracula*, 1897

MIDWAY upon the journey of our life
I found myself within a forest dark,
For the straightforward pathway had been lost.
Dante, *Inferno*

When Farmer Oak smiled, the corners of his mouth spread till they were within an unimportant distance of his ears, his eyes were reduced to chinks, and diverging wrinkles appeared round them, extending upon his countenance like the rays in a rudimentary sketch of the rising sun.
Thomas Hardy, *Far from the Madding Crowd*, 1874

In the country of Westphalia, in the castle of the most noble Baron of Thunder-ten-tronckh, lived a youth whom Nature had endowed with a most sweet disposition.
Voltaire, *Candide*, 1759

Mr. Phileas Fogg lived, in 1872, at No. 7, Saville Row, Burlington Gardens, the house in which Sheridan died in 1814. He was one of the most noticeable members of the Reform Club, though he seemed always to avoid attracting attention; an enigmatical personage, about whom little was known, except that he was a polished man of the world. People said that he resembled Byron--at least that his head was Byronic; but he was a bearded, tranquil Byron, who might live on a thousand years without growing old.
Jules Verne, *Around the World in Eighty Days*, 1873

`Christmas won't be Christmas without any presents,' grumbled Jo, lying on the rug.
Louisa May Alcott, *Little Women*, 1868

No one would have believed in the last years of the nineteenth century that this world was being watched keenly and closely by intelligences greater than man's and yet as mortal as his own; that as men busied themselves about their various concerns they were scrutinised and studied, perhaps almost as narrowly as a man with a microscope might scrutinise the transient creatures that swarm and multiply in a drop of water.
H. G. Wells, *The War of the Worlds*, 1898

Tall and burly, with features and skin hardened by exposure to the sun and winds of many climates, he looked like a man ready to face all hardships, equal to any emergency.
E. Phillips Oppenheim, *The Malefactor*

It was the evening on which MM. Debienne and Poligny, the managers of the Opera, were giving a last gala performance to mark their retirement.
Gaston Leroux, *The Phantom of the Opera*, 1911

Whanne that April with his shoures sote
The droughte of March hath perced to the rote.
Geoffrey Chaucer, *Canterbury Tales*, Unknown [Chaucer (1342 – 1400]

Whether I shall turn out to be the hero of my own life, or whether that station will be held by anybody else, these pages must show.
Charles Dickens, *David Copperfield*, 1850

The studio was filled with the rich odour of roses, and when the light summer wind stirred amidst the trees of the garden, there came through the open door the heavy scent of the lilac, or the more delicate perfume of the pink-flowering thorn.
Oscar Wilde, *The Picture of Dorian Gray*, 1891

I was born on the prairie and the milk of its wheat, the red of its clover, the eyes of its women, gave me a song and a slogan.
Carl Sandburg, *Cornhuskers*, 1918

Bizarre as was the name she bore, Kim Ravenal always said she was thankful it had been no worse.
Edna Ferber, S*how Boat*, 1926

He was an inch, perhaps two, under six feet, powerfully built, and he advanced straight at you with a slight stoop of the shoulders, head forward, and a fixed from-under stare which made you think of a charging bull.
Joseph Conrad, *Lord Jim*, 1900

I am a rather elderly man. The nature of my avocations for the last thirty years has brought me into more than ordinary contact with what would seem an interesting and somewhat singular set of men, of whom as yet nothing that I know of has ever been written:—I mean the law-copyists or scriveners. I have known very many of them, professionally and privately, and if I pleased, could relate divers histories, at which good-natured gentlemen might smile, and sentimental souls might weep. But I waive the biographies of all other scriveners for a few passages in the life of Bartleby, who was a scrivener the strangest I ever saw or heard of.
Herman Melville, *Bartleby, the Scrivener*, 1853

Buck did not read the newspapers, or he would have known that trouble was brewing, not alone for himself, but for every tide-water dog, strong of muscle and with warm, long hair, from Puget Sound to San Diego.
Jack London, *Call of the Wild*, (Serialized in *The Saturday Evening Post*, June 20-July 18, 1903)

The Daughter: " I'm getting chilled to the bone. What can Freddy be doing all this time? He's been gone twenty minutes."
George Bernard Shaw, *Pygmalion*, 1912 or 1913

I had this story from one who had no business to tell it to me, or to any other. I may credit the seductive influence of an old vintage upon the narrator for the beginning of it, and my own skeptical incredulity during the days that followed for the balance of the strange tale.
Edgar Rice Burroughs, *Tarzan of the Apes,* 1914

It is a truth universally acknowledged, that a single man in possession of a good fortune must be in want of a wife.
Jane Austen, *Pride and Prejudice*, 1813

When I wrote the following pages, or rather the bulk of them, I lived alone, in the woods, a mile from any neighbor, in a house which I had built myself, on the shore of Walden Pond, in Concord, Massachusetts, and earned my living by the labor of my hands only. I lived there two years and two months. At present I am a sojourner in civilized life again.
Henry David Thoreau, *Walden*, 1854

Whatever hour you woke there was a door shunting. From room to room they went, hand in hand, lifting here, opening there, making sure—a ghostly couple.
Virginia Woolf, *Monday or Tuesday*, 1921

He will hold thee, when his passion shall have
spent its novel force,
Something better than his dog,
A little dearer than his horse.

Tennyson, *Locksley Hall*, 1842

Mystery Authors' Trademarks

Some authors structure patterns in titles as their hallmarks:

- John D. MacDonald's Travis McGee series used color (*The Deep Blue Goodbye*).
- Sue Grafton is writing through the alphabet (*A is for 'Alibi'*).
- Janet Evanovich's bounty hunter series uses numbers (*One for the Money*).
- Lilian Braun uses cats (*The Cat Who Wasn't There*).
- Lawrence Block has the burglar series (*The Burglar in the Closet*).
- Philip Atlee has the word contract (*Paper Pistol Contract*).
- Erle Stanley Gardner always used cases (*The Case of the Angry Mourner*).
- Stuart M. Kaminsky uses red (*A Fine, Red Rain*).
- Ed McBain's Matthew Hope series uses nursery rhyme titles (*Jack and the Beanstalk*).
- Craig Rice played on phrases (*My Kingdom for a Hearse*).
- Edward D. Hoch's phrase is The Spy Who... (*The Spy Who Took the Long Route*).

Of course others use their character's name in the title: Heron Carvis (*Miss Seeton Draws the Line*); Leslie Charteris (*Saint Returns*); John Creasey (*Toff and the Terrified Taxman*; *Inspector West at Bay*); G.G. Fickling (*Gun for Honey*); Brett Halliday (*Violent World of Michael Shayne*); MacDonald Hastings (*Cork in the Doghouse*); Alan Hunter (*Gently Does It*); Michael Innes (*Appleby Talking*); H.R.F. Keating (*Inspector Ghote Plays a Joker*); Harry Kemelman (*Sunday the Rabbi Stayed Home*); J.J. Marric (*Gideon's Badge*); Anthony Morton (*Baron and the Unfinished Portrait*); Sax Rohmer (*Re-Enter Fu Manchu*); Georges Simenon (*Maigret and the Headless Corpse*); Arthur W. Upfield (*Bony Buys a Woman*); James Yaffe (*Mom Sings an Aria*).

Science Fiction Authors' Pseudonyms

Some of these SF authors write under more than one pseudonym,
as well as their own names.

Pseudonym	Author Name
Calvin M. Knox	Robert Silverberg
Walker Chapman	Robert Silverberg
A.A. Craig	Poul Anderson
Murray Leinster	William Fitzgerald Jenkins
John Riverside	Robert A. Heinlein
Edward Banks	Ray Bradbury
Leonard Douglas	Ray Bradbury
Walter Drummond	Robert Silverberg
George E. Dale	Isaac Asimov
Leonard Spaulding	Ray Bradbury
D.R. Banat	Ray Bradbury
William Anthony Parker White	Anthony Boucher
Sax Rohmer	Arthur Sarsfield Ward
Rog Phillips	Roger Phillips Graham
Caleb Saunders	Robert A. Heinlein
Lyle Monroe	Robert A. Heinlein
Christopher Bush	Charles Christmas Bush
Winston P. Sanders	Poul Anderson
William Elliott	Ray Bradbury
Lee Sebastian	David Osborne
Ivar Jorgenson	Robert Silverberg
Anson Macdonald	Robert A. Heinlein
Michael Karageorge	Poul Anderson
Charles Beaumont	Charles Nutt
C.J. Cherryh	Carolyn Janice Cherry
Voltaire	Francois-Marie Arouet

Banned Books

These books were banned at some time in the past,
usually by school systems:

The Adventures of Sherlock Holmes
The Adventures of Tom Sawyer and Huckleberry Finn
Alice's Adventures in Wonderland
The American Heritage Dictionary
Candide
Canterbury Tales
Catch-22
Catcher in the Rye
Citizen Tom Paine
The Clan of the Cave Bear
The Color Purple
Deliverance
The Diary of Anne Frank
Doctor Zhivago
East of Eden
A Farewell to Arms
For Whom the Bell Tolls
Forever Amber
From Here to Eternity
The Godfather
The Grapes of Wrath
The Great Gatsby
Hamlet
Hansel and Gretel
I, Claudius
King Lear
Lady Chatterley's Lover
Little Red Riding Hood
Madame Bovary
Merchant of Venice
Nineteen Eighty-Four

One Flew Over the Cuckoo's Nest
The Prince of Tides
Robin Hood
The Scarlett Letter
Sherlock Holmes
Silas Marner
Slaughterhouse-Five
Sophie's Choice
Ulysses
Where's Waldo?

Appendix B – Authors' Awards

Some authors have earned the following awards several times for different work. Particular authors have earned Life Achievement Awards: from World Fantasy, Horror Writers, Affaire de Coeur Hall of Fame, and Writers of the Future.

Several have been inducted into halls of fame: The Oklahoma Professional Writers Hall of Fame, Romance Writers of America Hall of Fame, and SF Hall of Fame.

We have a variety of awards—top ones such as the Pulitzer, Anthony, Hugo, Nebula, Sturgeon, Edgar, and the Agatha Award—as well as awards from such diverse groups as the Catholic Library Association, numerous universities, and libraries, and the New England Science Fiction Association.

The following is a list of the honors and recognition given to the authors showcased in *Hooking the Reader: Opening Lines that Sell*.

Achievement Award from Pacific Northwest Writers for
  Enhancing the State of Northwest Literature
Affaire de Coeur Silver Certificate
Agatha
Charles Angoff Award
Anlab -- The Annual Analog Readers Award
Anthony
Asimov's Reader's Choice Award
Associated Writing Program Award
Association of Jewish Libraries Award
The Aurora (Canadian Science Fiction and Fantasy Award)
Best Genre Fiction, A Top Five Romance –Library Journal
Best New Regency Author, Romantic Times

Best Novella, Midwest Fiction Writers
Best Regency Author
Best Regency Novel
Best Regency Romance
Best of the U.S. Small Presses
Best-selling Regency Author
Best-selling Regency Romance
Best-selling Story Collection
Best Time Travel
The Caldecott Medal
John W. Campbell Memorial Award
Canadian Science Fiction and Fantasy Award
Career Achievement Award for Regency Short Stories
Charlotte Award
Chesterfield Film Project
Chicago Foundation for Literature
The Christopher Medal
Colorado Library District
Colorado Romance Writers' Award of Excellence
Compton-Crook Award
CompuServe Science Fiction Forum's HOMer Award
Creative Writing Fellowship Grant, The Literary Review,
       Fairleigh-Dickinson University, Madison, NJ
Creative Writing Fellowship Grant, National Endowment for
       the Arts, Washington, DC
Crime Writers of Canada's Arthur Ellis Award
CWIP Award for Excellence in Adult Fiction
Distinguished Award, which is the highest award given by an
       SF society
Edgar
Arthur Ellis Award
Fiction Fellowship, Creative Artists Program Service (CAPS),
       New York State
Fiction Fellowship, New York Foundation for the Arts,
       New York City, NY
Fields Publications Teachers as Writers Award
Galaxy Award
John Gardner Fiction Fellow
Gold Letseizer Award
Golden Kite Award

Golden Leaf
Golden Scroll Independent Bookseller's Award
Great Lakes Book Award
Historical Romance Author of the Year
The Holt Medallion
L. Ron Hubbard Writers of the Future Contest
Hugo
Ignotus Award (Spanish Hugo)
Jewish Book Award
Aga Khan Prize for Fiction, 1996
Kiss of Death Award
Last Laugh Dagger awarded by the Crime Writers
    Association (Great Britain)
Le Grand Prix de l'Imaginaire (France's top SF award)
Lifetime Achievement Award, Waldenbooks
Literary Cavalcade Magazine
LOCUS
Macavity Award
"Maggie" (Best Southern Romance)
Midwest Fiction Writers
Mind Body Spirit Award for Excellence in Fiction
Mythopoeic Award
National Book Award
National Readers' Choice Award
Nebula
NEW YORK TIMES Notable Books of the Year
New York University Press Prize for Fiction
Northern Lights Award
Outstanding Regency Author
PI Writers of America/St. Martin's Press
"Porgy" award from West Coast Review of Books
Premio UPC de Ciencia Ficcion (Spain's top SF award)
Prix Apollo (France)
Prix du Roman d'Aventures (France)
Pulitzer
Regency Career Achievement Award
The Regency Plume's Award of Excellence
Reviewer's Choice
Rhysling
R*I*T*A Romance Writers of America Award
Rocky Mountain News "Unreal Worlds" Award for Best Horror
    Paperback
Romantic Times

Saguaro Screenplay Competition
Silver Plume
Skylark Award
Science Fiction and Fantasy Writers of America's Nebula
Award
Science Fiction Chronicle Reader Award
SFWA Grand Master
Seiun (Japan's top SF award)
Small Press Book Award
Southwest Book Award
Special Achievement Award for Sales Dominance in the
Category of Short Historical Romance
Bram Stoker Award
Sturgeon
Virginia Romance Writers
Frank Waters Award for Excellence in Writing
Willamette Writers Distinguished Northwest Writers Award
World Fantasy Award
Writer-in Residence, Woodstock Guild, Woodstock, NY
Writers of the Future
Writer's Voice Award

Index

Anderson, Poul 105
Asimov, Janet Jeppson 118
Authors' Awards 209
Ayres, E.C. 65

Balogh, Mary 24
Banned Books 207
Bayless, Martha 30
Bear, Greg 91
Beaumont, Nina 53
Blake, Jennifer 139
Brin, David 114
Brooks, Terry 55

Campbell, Harlen 81
Cats in the Pages 58
Chase, Robert 127
Chepaitis, B.A. 136
Cherryh, C.J. 69
Chittenden, Margaret (Meg) 62
Clarke, Sir Arthur C. 61
Cogan, Priscilla 5
Collaborative Teams—Mystery
    & Science Fiction
    Pseudonyms 58
Connelly, Michael 59

deCamp, L. Sprague 12
Delacroix, Claire 125
Dennis, Carol 28
Dietz, William C. 93

Eakins, Patricia 98
Emerson, Earl 2
Erickson, Lynn 97
Estleman, Loren 60

Finch, Sheila 143
Fontenay, Charles L. 105
Foster, Alan Dean 132
Freiman, Kate 160
Freireich, Valerie J. 104
Frommer, Sara Hoskinson 54

Gettler, Nina 53
Glover, Voyle A. 11
Goulart, Ron 71

Hager, Jean 5
Haldeman, Joe 102
Hall, James W. 23
Harper, Tara K. 180
Harris, Lee 173
Herbert, Brian 133
Hoch, Edward D. 91
Hovey, Joan Hall 131

Ing, Dean 176

Jacobs, Jonnie 64
James, Russell 44

Karr, Phyllis Ann 141
Kernaghan, Eileen 110
Kress, Nancy 49
Kushner, Ellen 187

Lance, Peter 3
Lansdale, Joe 148
Lawrence, J.A. 188
Lawrence, Martha C. 113
Leffers, Laura Lynn 174
Legg, John 45
Leiber, Justin 33
Levinson, Paul 46

Mackay, Scott 9
Mainstream Authors'
    Pseudonyms 79
McCaffrey, Anne 49
McKiernan, Dennis L. 73
Meredith, Marilyn 68
Michaels, Fern 158
Miller, Sasha 43
Moore, John 96
Morgan, Deborah 96
Multi-Genre Authors 52

Murphy, Shirley Rousseau 35
Mystery & Western Authors'
    Pseudonyms 187
Mystery Authors' Pseudonyms
    156
Mystery Authors' Trademarks
    205

Navarro, Yvonne 182
Niven, Larry 84
Nordley, G. David 115

Off the Classic Shelf 195
Off the Shelf 7, 16, 21, 25, 31,
    37, 47, 50, 55, 66, 70, 77,
    89, 93, 98, 108, 117, 121,
    128, 132, 137, 144, 151,
    154, 161, 166, 177, 184, 190

Paul, Barbara 92
Payne, Michael 69
Peltonen, Carla 97
Pence, Joanne 42
Pohl, Frederik 76
Pseudonyms 39
Putman, Eileen 168
Putney, Mary Jo 165

Reding, Jaclyn 87
Renfroe, Martha Kay 119
Roberts, Lora 146
Robinson, Peter 13
Romance Authors'
    Pseudonyms 186
Rosenblum, Mary 111

Sanders, William 83
Satterthwait, Walter 63

Sawyer, Robert J. 88
Schumacher, Aileen 163
Science Fiction Authors'
    Pseudonyms 206
Shames, Laurence 41
Sheriff, John 53
Smith, Sarah 124
Sperry, Ralph A. 19
Stabenow, Dana 5
Standiford, Les 18
Steinberg, Janice 15
Stratmann, Henry G., M.D. 27
Sumner, Mark 6
Swanton, Molly 97

Thompson, Frank 152
Toombs, Jane 159
Turney, Denise 75

van Belkom, Edo 19
Van Name, Mark L. 136
Van Nuys, Joan 60

Watt-Evans, Lawrence 107
Weinberg, Robert 83
Wentworth, K.D. 82
Wheat, Carolyn 103
Where the Sleuths Live 138
Williamson, Jack 20
Wilson, Charles 169
Wolfe, Gene 9
Wolzien, Valerie 127
Womack, Steven 130
Woods, Stuart 24
Wren, M.K. 119
Wright, Courtni 52

Yolen, Jane 33

About the Author

Award-winning author Shara Rendell-Smock has written *Living with Big Cats* and *Getting Hooked: Fiction's Opening Sentences 1950s-1990s*. Prior to writing fun books, she wrote more than thirty computer software manuals and numerous features both online and for newspapers, including the *Sarasota Herald-Tribune*.

She lives in Florida.